COURAG
After Fire

This extraor~~Laurence & Shirley Niederhofer~~ ~~ing from Iraq~~ ling from Iraq
and Afghani ~~In honor of financial support 2010~~ be successful.
As a Vietnam. I came home.
i have seen too many lives changed by war and not enough help after
returning home. As the former Secretary of the Department of Veterans
Affairs, I wish every returning veteran and their family would read it

> *The Honorable Anthony J. Principi*
> *Former Secretary of Veterans Affairs*

Courage After Fire is essential reading for all recent combat veterans, their
families and friends, military chaplains, employers, and clinicians at VA
hospitals and vet centers. Every recent combat vet and many of their family members will find a description of themselves to some degree in the
pages of this book. *Courage After Fire* provides a toolbox of useful insights
and coping exercises that can assist in saving a marriage or putting a veteran's life back on track. *Courage After Fire* should be issued to all returning veterans and family support groups.

> *Major Andy Johnson*
> *U.S. Army, Special Forces, OIF Veteran*

This wonderful book, starting with a heartfelt foreword by Senator Bob
Dole, serves as a virtual owner's manual for returning OEF/OIF war veterans. *Courage After Fire* is packed with practical information, culled from
hundreds of informed sources, and is written by three seasoned and sensitive practitioners and military veteran advocates. If you ever felt or said
you "supported the troops," no matter what your political view, show some
tangible support and buy this book for at least one returning veteran.

> *Professor Charles R. Figley, Ph.D.*
> *Director, Florida State University Traumatology Institute*

Courage After Fire offers both returning veterans and their families a clear understanding of the challenges that lie ahead and a practical guide for reintegration into home, work, and community. The scope of this book is supremely thorough and relevant, particularly to National Guard and Reservists. I am particularly pleased to see useful tips provided not only to family members, but employers as well, to assist them in their efforts to support our heroes of war. I highly recommend this book to service men and women of all branches, their families, and employers before, during, and after deployment.

Lieutenant General (Ret.) (RI) Reginald A. Centracchio
Former Commanding General of the Rhode Island National Guard

Courage After Fire provides critical information and practical skills for dealing with the emotional aftermath of recent wars. The specific focus on Iraq and Afghanistan veterans makes the material fresh and accessible. This book addresses a comprehensive range of areas of potential distress and concern for returning service men and women, giving them concrete and useful techniques for dealing with these issues in an active, empowering way. I feel certain that *Courage After Fire* will become an important source of information and self-healing for our returning troops.

Professor Bonnie L. Green, Ph.D.
Director, Georgetown University Center for Trauma and the Community

Returning home from Vietnam to my wife and family was both joyful and confusing. I felt estranged despite having a supportive community of friends and family. Although I already had set goals and a plan for my life, I had difficulty staying focused and on the right path. *Courage After Fire* provides a much needed roadmap to guide veterans and their families back to their life's path and the tools and strategies necessary to bring them truly home again.

Phillip Butler
Vietnam Veteran

Courage After Fire is the first comprehensive guide to recovery and reintegration for the men and women who have served in Afghanistan and Iraq. The authors bring their collective experience, wisdom, and compassion in their work with traumatized veterans and their families, and their exceptional abilities as educators to create a personal dialogue with those struggling to rebuild their lives after combat. *Courage After Fire* provides the tools to master a safe passage for all veterans on their journey home.

Charles R. Marmar, M.D.
Associate Chief of Staff and Director, PTSD Research Program
San Francisco Veterans Affairs Medical Center

Getting back to "normal" is one of the hardest things returning vets have to go through after coming home from war. No matter where you are in this process, *Courage After Fire* can help if you let it. Take what suggestions work for you from the many tips offered in this book—you may be surprised how much they can help.

Sergeant Victoria Steen
USAR, OIF-I (Honorably Discharged Iraq Veteran)

Courage After Fire is unique. It addresses the complete range of issues faced by returning National Guard and Reservist troops who are confronted with the difficulties of readjusting to their work and communities while, at the same time, dealing with the psychological ramifications of war.

William M. Coughran, Brigadier General
California Air National Guard, Ret.

Courage After Fire is an indispensable guide for troops returning from war. This book invites partners and family members to be a part of their veterans' healing process, which makes it all the more effective. I wish *Courage After Fire* were standard issue for all returning troops and for all health professionals, members of the clergy, and counselors who are in a position to support their transition home.

Robert-Jay Green, Ph.D., Distinguished Professor
California School of Professional Psychology
Alliant International University—San Francisco

COURAGE
After Fire

**Coping Strategies for Troops
Returning from Iraq and Afghanistan
and Their Families**

Keith Armstrong, L.C.S.W.
Suzanne Best, Ph.D.
Paula Domenici, Ph.D.

Foreword by Senator Bob Dole

Ulysses Press

"Exercise 10.3," from *Mastery of Your Anxiety and Panic*, 3rd edition, by David H. Barlow and Michelle G. Craske, © Oxford University Press, Inc. Used by permission of Oxford University Press, Inc.

Published by: Ulysses Press
             P.O. Box 3440
             Berkeley, CA 94703
             www.ulyssespress.com

For special orders from the publisher call 800-377-2542 x109

Library of Congress Control Number: 2005930011
ISBN10: 1-56975-513-2
ISBN13: 978-1-56975-513-6

Printed in Canada by Transcontinental Printing

20 19 18 17 16 15 14

Acquisitions editor: Ashley Chase
Editor: Richard Harris
Copyeditor: Mark Woodworth
Editorial and production staff: Lily Chou, Matt Orendorff,
    Kathryn Brooks
Index: Sayre Van Young
Cover design: Robles-Aragón
Cover credit: U.S. Army photo by SPC Daniel Kelley
Interior design: Leslie Henriques

Distributed by Publishers Group West

This book has been written and published strictly for informational purposes, and in no way should it be used as a substitute for consultation with professional therapists. All facts in this book came from scientific publications, personal interviews, published trade books, self-published materials by experts, magazine articles, and the personal-practice experiences of the authorities quoted or sources cited. The authors and publisher are providing you with information in this work so that you can have the knowledge and can choose, at your own risk, to act on that knowledge.

Contents

Foreword

by Senator Bob Dole

Coming back from a war is a longer journey than any plane flight home. It would be great if everything just snapped back together, the way it had always been—and if what happened in Tikrit stayed in Tikrit, for instance—but the truth is, returning from war is much more complicated than that. Digesting what you saw and what you missed and relating to your old world can be tough, even with terrific support. It feels unfair, considering the personal sacrifice. But fair or unfair, returning home is rarely what you imagine it will be.

I sustained my own injuries in World War II; some of my wounds were obvious, some were not. Some wounds healed more quickly than others. And though I was lucky to be surrounded by great doctors, wonderful family, and a more supportive community than anyone could reasonably ask for, that mental readjustment was no small task. I wish I could say the emotional and psychological recovery paled in comparison to the physical injuries, but that is not the case.

It can be an extremely tough thing to admit that the friends, family, and familiar places that kept us going while we were away somehow seem different, maybe a little off—especially when those fond memories and the new realities don't quite jibe and when our favorite parts of life seem oddly unfamiliar. And even though it might feel like a long time since something made us laugh, since we had a decent night's sleep, since we felt truly "home" in our own home—when so many people are worse off, it feels self-pitying, or weak, or cowardly to admit that we are not doing as well as we ought to be.

Fighting internal battles, when one has time and resources to do so, takes courage, just as signing up to serve your country, boarding a plane to Iraq or Afghanistan, risking one's own life to protect a fellow soldier, or venturing into hostile territory takes courage. It is not easy to consider that the dips in our quality of life are not acceptable, and that maybe we could use some new sources of strength and wisdom. It takes courage to make our own well-being the focus of attention—especially when self-sacrifice has become second nature.

I think this book, written specifically for OIF and OEF veterans, is a crucial tool for the men and women who have been serving our country so valiantly during these past years, even those with minimal readjustment difficulties. Each war is unique, each person's experience is different, but collectively we can help each other. The fund of knowledge put forth in *Courage After Fire* represents a sophisticated understanding of what it is like to be a soldier, and how the transition from military life to civilian life is inherently difficult.

This book does not treat readjustment challenges as a disorder, as a weakness, or as an artifact of selfishness. It simply addresses the challenges commonly faced by returning veterans, and provides thoughtful and practical strategies for dealing with them. Its three authors bring extensive experience to the table, having worked with veterans of my generation, your generation, and all those in between. That vast clinical experience, along with the authors' specialized research expertise in the field of combat stress, brings a new, welcome approach to addressing the problems that have always confronted veterans once tours of duty are completed.

I have seen too many brave men and women—selfless, smart, and strong to the core—lose their way after fighting in a war, and I confess that unnecessary suffering is difficult to stomach. Some veterans become delayed casualties of a war from which they returned home, in large part due to a misplaced selflessness that prevents them from putting resources into their own physical and mental health. And though we never could nor should forget our military experiences—the good times along with the traumatic times—we can harness those experiences into something that ultimately adds strength, perspective, and resilience to our lives. The sooner that process occurs, the easier it is for us and everyone around us.

In battle, courage means sacrificing our own well-being for our fellow soldiers and for our country. After battle, courage means concentrating on and being honest with ourselves, using all the tools we can gather to lead the best life we can, and, by example, giving something to those who will follow in our footsteps.

I thank you for your service to our country, and I sincerely encourage you to now focus on your own well-being.

Introduction

> "Courage: Mental strength to venture, persevere and withstand danger, fear or difficulty..."
>
> *(The Merriam-Webster Dictionary)*

If you're a veteran of Operation Iraqi Freedom (OIF) or Operation Enduring Freedom (OEF), we welcome you home and sincerely thank you for the time you served. Words can't convey the deep appreciation that we and other Americans across the country have for your valor, commitment, and hard work. While in harm's way, you endured many hardships, from constant threats and unpredictable crises to extreme temperatures, chaotic operations, absences from loved ones, and uncertainty about your return home. You have much of which you can be proud.

After the fanfare and welcome-home parties, though, you face the reality of trying to resume a "normal life." The courage and mental strength you need to transition home after your deployment ends often goes unrecognized. It takes fortitude and resilience to rejoin civilian life after war.

We've written this book to acknowledge the many challenges that veterans like you may face after returning home from Iraq and Afghanistan and to support your valiant efforts to readjust to your family, friends, work, and community. *Courage After Fire* is designed to help you understand common reactions that can occur after serving in a war zone and provide specific strategies to address them. This book focuses on the unique aspects of OIF and OEF, including the possibility of redeployment, the large number of US reservists and National Guard personnel participating in these operations, and the reality that, even with better medicine and body armor, many military service men and women taking part in OIF and OEF sustain physical and emotional wounds. Our goal is to offer help, hope, and inspiration on your journey home from war and during the months and years that follow.

This is the first book written directly for you, the veterans of OIF and OEF, to help you reclaim your life after deployment. It's for military service men and women of all backgrounds and all branches of the armed forces, including active-duty and discharged US Marines, Navy, Army, Coast Guard, and Air Force, as well as US reservists and National Guard. It's also for military service personnel who have remained stateside and are experiencing the effects of the war. In *Courage After Fire*, the term "veteran" is used to refer to all of you.

This book also is intended for spouses, partners, children, parents, brothers, sisters, grandparents, other relatives, and close friends—those who have kept things going on the home front and waited anxiously for your return. And it's for doctors, clinicians, counselors, health care providers, employers, colleagues, and others who may be asked to help you with your transition. As clinicians who have worked for years with veterans of various war eras, we know that war affects not only the troops but also their entire circle of family, friends, employers, and community.

We know the stigma people feel about asking for psychological help. And we know that seeking help can be especially hard for military service members. Some believe that it shows weakness, is shameful, or colors their military record. The truth is, getting help takes strength and courage. *Courage After Fire* can help you begin that process. We've also learned from working with veterans that identifying and addressing problems related to your war experience as soon as possible is vital to overcoming them. Reading this book today, and referring to it as needed in the future, will prove invaluable in the months and years to come.

For some, the information and strategies provided here will be all you need to make a successful return to postdeployment life. For others, *Courage After Fire* will be just the beginning on the road to seeking help. This book includes tips and strategies that can open the door for you to have a dialogue with yourself and those close to you about what you're going through and how to ease your transition. This book can help you and your loved ones determine whether you should seek professional help and identify the resources available to you. Sometimes your loved ones notice the effects of your war experience before you do, and this book can be a guide for them to help you. If you're already working with a therapist, this book may help with your therapy.

Your military service probably included life-threatening and traumatic events, many of which were unthinkable before war. For instance, the range of wartime experiences can include not only attacks from the enemy but also sexual assaults from fellow service members. Sexual trauma against both women and men is finally being recognized as a real problem in the military. Although military sexual trauma is not the focus of this book, many of the suggestions offered here for coping with combat-related trauma can be helpful for dealing with sexual trauma as well. Likewise, though this book isn't specifically intended to help veterans suffering from physical disabilities that resulted from war, it does present ways to handle the psychological complications that often come with physical injuries.

Each person reading this book has been affected differently by his or her wartime experience, even if it was the same operation. You and your fellow service members had different reasons for going to war and various expectations about what war would be. You had different family and social lives before being deployed, and you're returning to different situations. All these things impact how you respond to deployment, view your military service, and readjust to postdeployment life today. As you use this book, certain chapters will apply to your situation, while others won't. Choose those sections that apply to you. You may not need to read the whole book.

Chapter 1, "Reactions to War," reviews positive effects of your war-zone service and the common problems associated with it, including anxiety, anger, alcohol and drug use, and depression. It will help you understand why and how these problems develop.

Armed with this understanding, in Chapters 2 and 3 you'll find tips and exercises to help you manage these difficulties so that you can "get on" with your life. In *Chapter 2*, "Strengthening Your Mind and Body," you'll identify and build on skills you already have with a series of relaxation exercises aimed at reducing war-related stress. We also review techniques for taking "stronger" care of yourself, including tips for sleep, exercise, and healthy eating. Then in *Chapter 3*, "Coping Strategies," we'll look at proven strategies to directly combat and take control of your unwanted war reactions.

Chapter 4, "Grief and Loss," addresses the many losses that you may have experienced during war—such as the loss of innocence, a close friend, or a physical ability. This chapter describes thoughts and feelings that veterans typically have after a wartime loss and discusses strategies for coping with these emotional aftereffects.

Chapter 5, "Changed Views of Self, Others, and the World," looks at how your ideas about issues such as safety, trust, control, power, and relationships may have changed because of your deployment. It invites you to think about whether you see yourself, others, and the world differently since being at war. If so, how are these changes affecting you today? If you feel that your changed views are getting in the way of your readjustment at home, this chapter offers strategies that can help.

In *Chapter 6,* "Returning to Civilian Life," you'll find suggestions for readjusting to work, school, and the community, including practical advice about how to respond to difficult questions that people may ask about your war experience. This chapter also tells employers how to help returning veterans like you reenter the workforce.

Turning next to your family, *Chapter 7,* "Restoring Family Roles and Relationships," will help you see and understand changes that have occurred at home during your absence and learn a number of strategies to help you adjust to these changes. There you'll find tips on how to talk to friends and family members about your war experience and ways to reconnect with loved ones, including advice about reuniting with children.

Finally, the "Resources" section provides a practical list of books and websites where you can get further information on specific issues related to your readjustment. These resources include veterans' organizations, employment links, and support groups.

The examples and anecdotes in this book are based on our clinical work with returning veterans from both OIF and OEF. They have been modified so they don't reveal any veteran's identity. They not only illustrate problems that you may be experiencing but also provide concrete examples of healthy ways to cope with them. Each coping strategy or exercise includes step-by-step procedures to make it easy for you to try it and see if it helps you. Use the ideas provided in this book to build your own coping toolbox by blending them with the skills you already possess. At the end of each chapter we provide coping tips for your partners, family members, and close friends. Use them as a springboard for working together as you—and they—adjust to your return home.

We hope the information and suggestions in *Courage After Fire* will inspire you and your loved ones to persevere and withstand the difficulties you may be experiencing. Here at home, as well as over there, how you deal with the effects of war is a tribute to your bravery.

Reactions to War

Steve, a Sergeant in the Marine Reserves, came home to San Diego four months ago from a tour in Iraq where he and his fellow Marines transported and guarded ammunition. He has returned to his job as a carpenter and is spending his free time with friends and family, who are very happy to have him home. In fact, a celebration of his return was held on the street where he grew up, with old friends welcoming him back.

In some ways, Steve misses being in Iraq—the sense that he was serving not just his community but his entire country, and the closeness he felt with his buddies. But he appreciates his freedom as a civilian and is enjoying the things that he was unable to have or do when he was overseas. He feels closer to his family than ever before. Steve is talking more about his thoughts and feelings to his wife and his father, a Vietnam veteran. He has a newfound appreciation for his children and really enjoys his time with them.

Although when he first returned home he had some difficulty sleeping and felt a bit on edge, especially in crowds, he is sleeping well now and feels like he is "pretty much back to normal."

But Steve knows that he has been changed by his experience in Iraq. He feels much more confident in his ability to accomplish difficult tasks and is no longer afraid to accept challenging jobs. He also feels more respected in his community

and is more comfortable attending social events than he did
before he deployed to Iraq.

* * *

Eric, a Captain in the Air Force who flew helicopters in Fallujah
in a combat support role, has returned home after sustaining a
leg injury when his chopper was shot down. He's no longer on
active duty. What troubles him most now is that he fears going
to sleep because he has nightmares almost every night and he
can't shake the feeling that if he doesn't stay awake, "something
bad might happen."

Eric has given up on anything related to the military: He has
put away his uniform and ceased contact with others in his unit.
He stays at home most of the time. But he can't stop thinking
about Iraq. Images of the chopper accident pop into his head
every day. He has lost interest in flying, which he once loved, as
well as in spending time with friends.

These are just two examples of returning veterans and their reactions to their war experiences. Although Steve experienced some
uncomfortable feelings after returning from Iraq, over time he has
adjusted to being home. His initial "edginess" has all but disap-
peared. In fact, since returning home, Steve has found that his
work and relationships have improved. Eric, by contrast, has
become fearful, angry, depressed, and withdrawn. He wishes that
he had never gone to Iraq and wonders if he will ever "get over
it."

Like Steve, many veterans return from their time at war with
a sense of accomplishment and only a few difficulties that will
simply fade away with time. But it is not unusual for war veterans
like Eric to develop problems that interfere with their ability to
"return to normal." Let's look at some of the positive effects of
your war-zone service and then at some of the more common
problematic reactions to war. In this chapter, you'll see why and
how these problems develop.

Positive Effects of War

Many veterans, like Steve, talk proudly of their time overseas and the ways in which it changed them for the better. Serving your country in a war effort can leave you with a sense of honor and self-respect that's hard to come by in most civilian occupations. Working closely with others during life-threatening war situations helps to create a bond that is nearly impossible to forge in other environments. Some veterans may even have surprised themselves with the things they were able to accomplish under difficult circumstances in Iraq or Afghanistan. For others, recalling how they performed their duties while under fire gives them courage to face difficult situations and challenges at home. Their community may celebrate their return and hold them in higher esteem because of the tremendous sacrifices they made. And for many veterans, even though it was extremely difficult to leave their home, job or school, and family for war, their sacrifice has given them a sense of pride and commitment that can't be easily described.

Negative Effects of War

Unfortunately, though many veterans returning from OEF or OIF experience positive changes such as those mentioned above, others will be negatively affected by war. The sections that follow will address some of the more common problems seen in returning Iraq and Afghanistan veterans: anxiety, posttraumatic stress, panic attacks, phobias, anger, substance abuse, and depression.

Anxiety

Jeff, an Army reservist who served two back-to-back tours in Afghanistan hunting down Taliban soldiers in the vast and desolate mountain region, has recently returned to his hometown of Chicago. A lifelong White Sox fan, he looked forward with excitement to seeing his first postdeployment game. But as Jeff walked toward the stadium with the crowds of fellow fans, he found himself becoming increasingly nervous. His muscles began to tense and his breathing and heart rate became more rapid. By the time he got to his seat and saw the sea of screaming, cheering people, he was dizzy, nauseated, and trembling. He turned and ran to his car where, once inside, he began to feel better. Jeff has not been to a game since.

Since returning home to Valparaiso, Indiana, from Iraq, **Andria**, a Marine reservist, can't sleep. She dreams about a suicide bomber who detonated 20 yards from her and several other Marines. Although she was not hurt, Andria was splattered by the bomber's remains, and two of her buddies were seriously injured. She is trying to keep as busy as possible with work, night classes, and various hobbies to avoid bad thoughts about this experience. She drinks quite heavily at night to fall asleep.

Toby is a Guardsman who has just returned home to Sandusky, Ohio, from an 18-month tour in Iraq, after being extended twice. He served in the transportation unit there and went on multiple convoys, constantly under threat of fire and bombings. Since returning home, Toby has had a hard time driving, especially on streets where there are many cars and pedestrians. He now avoids main thoroughfares, runs errands on off-hours, and drives much faster than is safe so he can get to his destination as quickly as possible.

Each of these veterans suffers from anxiety caused by life-threatening war-zone experiences. But during their deployment, many of the same behaviors and reactions that now interfere with their lives were helpful, if not downright necessary to their survival.

After months of traversing wide-open, desolate spaces, knowing that the enemy could be around any turn or behind any hill, Jeff became acutely aware of every human sound or movement. To continue with her duties that required interaction with Iraqi citizens, Andria used every means possible to push away her memory of the suicide bomber. To survive the Iraq convoy runs, Toby had to drive as fast as possible, alert to every pedestrian and car that could represent a potential sniper or bomber.

Although these survival reactions served a great purpose in the war, they became so routine that now, even though these veterans are home and in nonthreatening environments, they simply can't turn off their alert systems. What was once a survival tool is now an anxious habit.

As these examples show, anxiety comes in different forms and can range from discomfort to full-blown panic attacks. In the next three sections, we'll look at the most common anxiety reactions experienced by returning OIF and OEF veterans: posttraumatic stress, panic attacks, and phobias.

Posttraumatic Stress

Steve and Eric reacted very differently to having been at war. One reason may be that Eric had a life-threatening experience when he went down in his chopper. Steve's duties handling ammunition were sometimes dangerous too, but he never felt directly threatened. His experience in Iraq would not normally be considered "traumatic."

But like Eric, many veterans who served in Iraq and Afghanistan experienced at least one traumatic event there: a sudden, overwhelmingly stressful experience. It may have involved a physical threat or danger that caused strong feelings of fear. It may have involved witnessing a tragedy, such as a death, that caused intense horror or helplessness. These situations overwhelm a person's natural coping abilities. Sometimes even just hearing about such incidents involving someone you know or feel close to can be a traumatic experience.

People commonly have certain reactions after experiencing a traumatic event:

- Night sweats and nightmares directly or symbolically related to the traumatic experience
- Unwanted daytime memories, thoughts, or images of the traumatic event, like a disturbing movie playing over and over again in your mind
- Flashbacks or feeling like you're reliving the traumatic event
- Strong physical and emotional reactions to things that remind you of the traumatic experience
- Avoiding thoughts, people, places, or things related to the traumatic event
- Avoiding talking about the traumatic event
- Disconnecting from friends or family and not being able to feel close to others
- Feeling emotionally numb
- Sleep problems
- Anger, irritability, and fear of becoming violent
- Jumpiness, being easily startled, and hypersensitivity to noises
- Hyperalertness, being constantly on guard, and looking around for possible danger
- Problems with concentration, attention, or memory

Veterans' reactions to traumatic war incidents vary. Some go through a traumatic event without being overwhelmed by intense emotions because they feel trained to handle it. Others may recover quickly from the first incident but have problems after an accumulation of incidents. In some cases, problems may not surface until months after a veteran returns from war.

Whatever the case, if you've been experiencing some of the trauma responses listed above for more than one month since returning home, you may be experiencing posttraumatic stress. Veterans who have been through previous traumas before going to war may be especially vulnerable to developing posttraumatic stress after their wartime experience.

WHAT IS POSTTRAUMATIC STRESS?

As a traumatic event occurs, the mind registers "DANGER" and the body immediately responds by going into survival mode. To protect yourself and those around you, you must be prepared to either *fight* or *flee* the threatening situation. Your heart rate increases, sending more blood to your arms and legs in preparation for action; your breathing becomes more rapid so you can take in more oxygen; and your pupils constrict so you can focus more intently on the source of the danger. These reactions help you harness all your strength and energy to act. You can suddenly run faster than you ever have, carry a buddy twice your weight to safety, or focus on your target when all around you is chaos.

AROUSAL

> **Damita**, an Army reservist from New York City, noticed that since returning from Iraq, when she is out walking and sees people dressed with turbans or hears Arabic being spoken, she begins sweating and becomes panicky. Her heart races, and she instinctively puts her hand in her pocket, as if ready to pull out a weapon for self-protection.

When a trauma survivor develops posttraumatic stress, it is because he or she keeps on operating in survival mode long after the threat or trauma has ended. Posttraumatic stress sufferers—not only combat veterans, but others such as victims of sexual assault or natural disaster—stay constantly aroused, as if emotionally and physically prepared to fight or flee *at all times*. This arousal, which was useful and maybe even vital at the time of the trauma, is now a source of distress. "Exaggerated" arousal is responsible for a variety of posttraumatic stress symptoms, including jumpiness, anger and irritability, sleep difficulties, and poor concentration.

Posttraumatic stress has been called a disorder of emotional *and* physical arousal. That is, the trauma affects not only the mind but also the body, even when there is no direct physical injury, and causes both mind and body to be on constant alert. When exaggerated arousal, or being "amped," is constant, situations that remind you of the trauma can cause a racing heart and rapid breathing like those you experienced at the time of the trauma. These situations, which cause the body to go on "full alert," are called "triggers." Triggers can come through any of the senses and include sounds, sights, tastes, and smells. Other physiological reactions to triggers may include trembling, sweating, lightheadedness or dizziness, tingling in your legs or arms, nausea, or tightness in your chest or stomach. Specific reminders that may trigger responses for returning veterans include:

- Going to drills on weekends (If you are still in the National Guard or Reserves)
- Watching current news about the wars in Iraq and Afghanistan
- Hearing about deaths of military service members in Iraq and Afghanistan
- Seeing certain vehicles that remind you of those driven by Iraqis or Afghanis who shot at you
- Being around children who remind you of kids in the war zone
- Seeing or hearing helicopters
- Smelling oil or gas that reminds you of burning buildings and carnage
- Certain types of weather or terrain that remind you of Iraq or Afghanistan
- Being scheduled for redeployment or being redeployed
- Seeing Arab-looking people who remind you of the enemy

An anniversary date of a traumatic event also can bring back thoughts, feelings, and physical reactions related to the trauma. For instance, a veteran may experience an "anniversary reaction" or an increase in posttraumatic stress symptoms at Thanksgiving, as she recalls a mortar blast that happened on Thanksgiving Day, killing one of her buddies. Anniversary reactions can cause intense peaks in anxiety or depression and may occur even before you consciously remember that a particular traumatic event happened on that date.

AVOIDANCE

Matt discovers that each time he drives on certain busy streets, he quickly is reminded of all the times when he was shot at by Iraqis while driving a truck on Baghdad's principal streets. He trembles with anxiety whenever he is forced to slow down in traffic. So Matt avoids main thoroughfares and steers clear of highways altogether.

It is understandable that Matt would want to avoid busy streets, because they trigger uncomfortable reactions. People who suffer from posttraumatic stress avoid triggers because they believe that if they're not reminded of their traumatic experience, they'll get over it more quickly. But this natural avoidance tendency actually works to worsen your symptoms by reinforcing the idea that you're still in danger—that you're living in a war zone. Avoiding reminders of your war experience keeps you from learning that in reality they aren't dangerous; they are just triggers to a memory of a past incident that was traumatic. Besides, avoiding triggers can interfere with your ability to work effectively, participate in activities, or enjoy your relationships now that you're home. Some avoidance strategies, such as excessive drinking, use of drugs, and risk-taking such as reckless driving, overeating, or overworking, may even be harmful.

Panic Attacks

Glen used to be an avid runner, but since returning home to Grand Rapids, Michigan, from a tour in Afghanistan he has given up running and just about every other form of physical activity.

> When he exercises, he experiences a sudden attack of anxiety
> that is so intense he fears that he is losing his mind.

Another anxiety condition common in veterans returning from Iraq and Afghanistan that can be experienced either with or without posttraumatic stress is panic attacks. Although the term "panic attack" is popularly used to mean the kind of anxiety or stress you experience when taking an exam or losing your wallet, a true panic attack is an extreme anxiety reaction brought on by a sense of intense fear. During a panic attack, your body goes into *hypersurvival* mode. Your heart begins to pound so hard that you fear you're having a heart attack. Your breathing becomes so rapid that you start to hyperventilate. Your head pounds, and you begin to feel dizzy, sick to your stomach, and disoriented. Some people get attacks so intense that they fear they might go crazy or even die.

True panic attacks do not occur in response to a real danger at the time. They're triggered by the physical sensations associated with the body's danger alert system or survival response. Just as you can feel threatened by your memories of war, you can also feel that physical reactions similar to those you experienced during times of danger at war mean that you are currently under threat. For instance, you climb a short flight of stairs to get to a friend's apartment and your heart begins to beat more rapidly. By the time you get to the top of the stairs you're sweating, shaking, and having difficulty breathing, and you fear that you may lose control. You are having a panic attack brought on by an increased heart rate, the same kind of physical sensation you felt when in danger in Iraq or Afghanistan.

AVOIDANCE

As with posttraumatic stress, panic attacks can cause a person to avoid anything that they believe may lead to another attack. But with panic attacks it's often not so easy to know what has caused the symptoms to occur, and people frequently describe their attacks as "coming out of the blue." Yet in their effort to put an end to these attacks, panic sufferers avoid any situation or place that they think may cause one. One person may avoid bus stops, for instance, because she once had a panic attack while waiting for the bus. Another may avoid driving because he experienced a panic attack while sitting in traffic. But as with posttraumatic stress, this avoidance actually causes the attacks to continue, because the body and mind do not have a chance to learn that these experiences don't signal present danger.

Phobias

Other fears that can develop out of war may be very simple and specific. These circumscribed fears are called "phobias."

AGORAPHOBIA

A fear of open or crowded spaces is called "agoraphobia." It can develop because people who experience panic attacks tend to avoid situations or places that they think may bring on another attack.

For instance, Jeff started out by avoiding White Sox games, but as time went on, he began to avoid other situations as well. He felt anxious when entering a movie theater, then later felt nervous that week at a shopping mall, so he decided to rent movies at home and shop online instead. Then he realized that he felt uncomfortable while shopping at the grocery store. Fearing that this might build into a panic attack, he began having his groceries delivered. Soon Jeff had restricted his activities to work and home. When he needed to venture out, he did it during off-hours when places would be less crowded. In addition to panic attacks, Jeff now was suffering from agoraphobia. Jeff's Afghanistan deployment had placed him in wide-open, unpopulated, yet dangerous terrain. That made it hard for him to readjust to civilian life in a crowded, urban city.

Agoraphobia commonly affects people who suffer from repeated panic attacks. It can occur with or without other anxiety conditions such as posttraumatic stress. Although most military service members returning from Iraq or Afghanistan don't develop agoraphobia, many complain of feeling uncomfortable or on edge in their own hometowns, especially in places that are crowded or densely built.

OTHER COMMON PHOBIAS

Besides agoraphobia, veterans may return with other phobias, such as an intense fear of flying, spiders, overpasses, or fire. Specific fears like these can develop from things that happened while deployed, such as being bitten by a camel spider or hit by a sniper from an overpass. With all phobias, including agoraphobia, the need to avoid the feared object or situation keeps the fear alive. By avoiding all flying, for example, you don't have the chance to learn that not all planes and helicopters are dangerous.

With each of these anxiety conditions, *avoidance* is the element that drives the problem. So reducing the need to avoid is key. Chapter 3 will provide you with simple but effective techniques for turning down your alert signal and learning once again how to relax.

Anger

Bill is a 24-year-old Army soldier from Togus, Maine, who recently returned from a 14-month tour in Iraq, where he was stationed in Fallujah. Bill had started a new job with a very competitive company just before getting his orders to deploy. He was frustrated that he had to leave at such a crucial time in his career. In Iraq, with little sleep and in all types of extreme weather, Bill spent nearly every day of his tour searching out and fighting insurgents with what he and his buddies considered to be "crap" equipment and supplies. As his exhaustion grew, he could feel himself becoming more and more angry. "What's wrong with these people—can't they see that we're here to help?" he'd say. After a few months, the only thing that kept him going was his anger.

Then one day he received word that his mother back in Maine had become ill with breast cancer. He asked to go on emergency leave to be with her, but his request was denied. He flew into a rage but was talked out of hurting the C.O. who denied his request. Luckily, Bill's mother recovered.

But now that he's back home, Bill has little patience for his family, his coworkers, or the military in general. He has already gotten into three fights and been put in jail overnight for one of them. According to Bill, "Each of those guys asked for it. Besides, fighting makes me feel alive and gives me a good rush."

WHAT IS ANGER?

Anger is a natural human emotion that all people experience. It's related to the biological survival mechanism that prepares us to fight or flee when our minds register danger by increasing our breathing, heart rate, and blood flow. In a war zone, military service members use this survival mechanism and their military training to carry out their duties. And for many, these duties include fighting. Anger is a complex combination of physical arousal, thoughts, and emotions that can show itself through a variety of responses:

- *Physical arousal*: Increased heart rate, blood flow, and breathing. Tensed muscles, narrowed vision, heightened senses, clenched fists, furrowed brow, sweating, flushed cheeks, shaking
- *Thoughts*: Negative thoughts about a situation (such as "This is a hopeless assignment"; "That C.O. is out to get me"; "I'm going to kill that guy")

- *Emotions*: Feelings ranging from frustration and irritability to intense rage
- *Behaviors*: Actions driven by angry feelings, such as acting aggressively or violently toward others or yourself, avoiding people, or yelling at people

ANGER THAT IGNITES AT WAR

Do you have to experience anger in order to fight? No, not necessarily. But war is a prime place for it to emerge. Anger is a natural response that can protect you from feeling paralyzed and, in fact, may have helped keep you alive in a war zone, where your life and the lives of your buddies were threatened on a daily basis. Maybe you had to work under extreme conditions such as searing heat or flash floods. Maybe poor equipment and body armor, limited supplies, or inadequate training made accomplishing your day-to-day duties nearly impossible. Or maybe, like Bill, the seemingly never-ending stream of insurgents, snipers, and suicide bombers simply wore you down, leaving you feeling hopeless and frustrated. The extra stress of hearing about crises at home and not being there to help may have been the final straw.

War-zone situations like these can make you feel powerless because you can't change the situation you are faced with. Anger is a common reaction to feelings such as helplessness or fear, the confusion that can come from finding yourself at war, and other emotions such as feeling betrayed or guilty. Anger causes your physical arousal to go up, so it can help you feel more powerful at the moment. This feeling, especially in the face of danger, is addictive, and it can lead to more frequent and intense anger reactions that eventually permeate your entire life. Using your anger to hurt others can also make you feel powerful, dominating, and indestructible.

ANGER AT HOME

Now that you're home, you may find that you get angry more often than you did before you left for war. Your reactions may be more extreme than they used to be. You may feel that you're losing control when you get angry and feel unable to rein in your anger when you want to. Reactions that may have been natural and useful during war can interfere with your day-to-day life at home. You may frighten your family, have arguments at work, develop health problems such as high blood pressure, or even end up in jail—all because of the way your anger seems to take over. The important thing to remember is that the anger you felt at war helped you to feel a greater sense of power and control. But now that you're home and are no longer under threat, this anger is no longer useful. In fact, *it* may be controlling *you*.

Substance Use

Joe, a 23-year-old soldier from Abilene, Kansas, can't keep his mind off the war. Although he occasionally drank with his friends in high school before entering the service, and drank while he was stationed in Iraq, since his tour of duty he is finding a reason to drink whenever he can. He is consuming a fifth of Jack Daniels a day. He also has started using speed when he goes to bars because it makes him feel more confident and powerful. When he gets home, he winds down by smoking marijuana, which he believes helps him relax and sleep. In the morning, he quickly takes a shot of Jack Daniels to steady his tremor and relieve his hangover. His parents have mentioned their concern about his drinking and suggested that he go see someone at the VA, but Joe thinks that if they just left him alone he would be fine.

Danny, a reservist and married father of two from Selma, Alabama, came home from the war and immediately started back at his job as a firefighter. During his off-duty hours, he goes out and gets drunk one or two times a week, pounding down 8 to 10 beers in as little as two hours because it helps him feel less "jumpy." Because of his drinking, he's late to work a lot and has missed many family events he was committed to attend. Before the war, he was an exemplary firefighter, never late, and a very involved father. But now he's irritable with his family and feels on edge most of the time. His wife is unsure how to talk to him about her concerns.

Jane, a 32-year-old single reservist from Fresno, California, returned home from her tour of duty in Iraq. She occasionally has a drink with friends, mainly as a way to catch up, but also to avoid uncomfortable feelings from her war-zone experience. However, Jane's drinking doesn't interfere with the rest of her life. She's doing well in school, and is enjoying being with family and friends.

SUBSTANCE USE IN THE WAR ZONE

One typical way to cope with the daily stresses of a war operation is to use drugs or alcohol. Drinking after a difficult day is a common way for you to unwind, relax, and enjoy some downtime with fellow service members. It may also provide a distraction from an especially bad experience. Or maybe it just gives you something to do. But regular drinking or drug use over the course of deployment can make you believe that when you're under stress you need to use substances to cope. This belief has serious consequences. Too much use while deployed may also dull your ability to perform your job under stress. Alcohol or drug use in the war zone can pave the way for further use (or abuse) at home.

SUBSTANCE USE AT HOME

Many veterans returning from Iraq or Afghanistan will use alcohol or drugs for a variety of reasons, such as these:

- To avoid thinking about past events from war that are still upsetting

- To avoid troubling or disturbing feelings like depression, guilt, shame, or grief related to war
- To take the edge off being physically amped
- To help with sleep and nightmares
- To "loosen up" and have fun, making it easier to talk about things that happened during war
- To feel powerful and invincible
- To fit in

Drugs or alcohol can make socializing with others, especially civilians, seem easier. Veterans who are feeling misunderstood or having a hard time fitting in are likely to use the alcohol or drugs that others in their social group are using. Other veterans use methamphetamine to achieve the same adrenaline rush they had while in combat. They feel more alive and will use speed to help them in public situations like bars or to enhance sexual activity.

COPING BY USING ALCOHOL OR DRUGS

It's no wonder that many veterans returning from Iraq and Afghanistan cope by using alcohol or drugs. But alcohol and drugs are seductive. When you drink or use drugs, you may believe that you have successfully gotten through a difficult situation or beaten a problem. You may rely on these crutches more and more to cope with day-to-day stressors you're faced with at home or to deal with powerful memories from war. But this is just an illusion.

In reality, substances only offer a way to *avoid* dealing with uncomfortable situations, memories, or feelings. Remember, avoidance, which also fuels such problems as phobias, panic attacks, and posttraumatic stress, drives alcohol or drug use.

Using drugs or alcohol can also increase feelings of depression, causing you to feel more negative about yourself and your situation. And since substances tend to lose their effectiveness over time, you increase how much you drink or use drugs. So while you still have your original problems, you also create a whole new set of problems for yourself and your family and friends. In the short run you find relief, but in the long run you make it a lot harder to get help for yourself.

If you grew up in a family where alcohol or drugs were used as a way to "deal with" difficult or traumatic situations, you're more likely to use them yourself in similar situations. Maybe you used drugs or alcohol to excess before entering the military. This pattern will increase the likelihood that you'll turn to them after returning from Iraq or Afghanistan.

So should you refrain from using alcohol or drugs altogether? No, not necessarily.

For some, like Jane, it's possible to drink without its interfering with your life or your ability to face problems as they arise. But if you're wondering whether you or someone you care about has a drug or alcohol problem, here are some red flags to watch out for:

SIGNS OF SUBSTANCE ABUSE/DEPENDENCE

- Failing to fulfill responsibilities at home, school, or work because of alcohol or drug use
- Using alcohol or drugs in situations where it's dangerous (such as driving a car or using machinery when high or intoxicated)
- Getting into fights or experiencing legal problems because of alcohol or drugs
- Continuing to use even though it's causing problems (say, getting into arguments with family members because of alcohol or drug use, getting fired, or failing in school)
- Needing more of the drug or alcohol to feel high

- Having withdrawal symptoms when you're not using (such as alcohol-withdrawal symptoms like sweating, trembling, sleep problems, nausea, or anxiety)
- Using drugs or alcohol to keep from having withdrawal symptoms (like Joe's having a drink in the morning to help with a tremor)
- Giving up important activities in order to drink or get high
- Spending a lot of time or money to get the drug or alcohol

In Joe's situation, he's clearly showing signs of alcohol dependence and is probably also abusing marijuana and speed, while Danny might be seen as someone who binge drinks or abuses alcohol. In both cases, these veterans are putting themselves at risk for making their war-related problems worse. In Joe's case, the evidence is overwhelming that he has a problem, though he may not admit it. Danny's situation, on the other hand, is less dramatic. He doesn't think substances are causing him that much difficulty. However, in reality, the substances probably are hurting him and his family more than he thinks. In the long run, if he keeps this pattern up, there could be very serious consequences. In Chapter 4, we'll talk about how to get help if you have a drug or alcohol problem.

Depression

As a Navy medic based at a military hospital outside Fallujah, **Mitch** treated Marines with extensive injuries. Some of them ended up dying. Before his deployment, Mitch had pitched for his Catskill, New York, softball team and enjoyed watching sporting events and going fishing with his friends. But since his return, Mitch doesn't seem to enjoy much of anything, not even watching or playing sports. He doesn't return his friends' calls. In fact, he has a hard time getting out of bed. Mitch thinks often about how he "failed" those Marines who died and how he's a "failure" today, unable to find work no matter how hard he tries.

DEPRESSION AND TRAUMA

Most anyone would recognize that Mitch is depressed—but what is depression, actually? Like anger, depression is not just a feeling, it's a complex blend of thoughts, behaviors, emotions, and physiological changes that work together to keep a person "stuck" in a dark mood:

- *Thoughts:* "I'm a failure," "Nothing ever goes right for me"
- *Behaviors:* Inactivity, problems sleeping (oversleeping, waking too early), isolation
- *Emotions:* Feelings ranging from being "down" to wanting to die
- *Physiological:* Loss or gain in appetite, loss in sex drive, fatigue

Just as the increased physical arousal that comes with being aggressive can cause anger to spiral upward, decreased physical arousal can cause a downward cycle into inactivity and deeper depression. Being in a depressed mood makes it hard to enjoy many activities, and the less active you are, the more likely you are to feel depressed. A depressed mood can also cause you to see things more negatively, making it harder to motivate yourself to participate in activities. And the less active you are, the more time you have to dwell on negative thoughts about yourself, making you feel even more depressed.

The following model, taken from the work of Dr. Richard Bryant, illustrates this Cycle of Depression:

Depression can be brought on by trauma or ongoing stress. For people who have experienced war-zone trauma and the stress of deployment, it can be a very real problem. Depression often

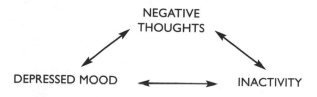

comes from loss—loss of a buddy, a physical ability, a limb, a relationship, or a job. It can also come from feeling helpless or overwhelmed, when a situation is beyond your ability to cope. Like, for instance, when things go wrong at home while you're deployed overseas. War-zone experiences can also lead to depression if they cause you to feel guilt or shame, or to see yourself or the world in a more negative light.

SUICIDE WATCH

For a few returning OEF and OIF veterans, the downward cycle of depression has led them to think about suicide, and some have even killed themselves. It's fairly common for depressed people, particularly those who have been traumatized by war, to think about death. But if you're having thoughts about hurting or killing yourself, you must get help *immediately*. The same is true if someone else you know is talking about suicide. Turn to the "Resources" section for information on how to find help and support in your area.

TIPS FOR PARTNERS, FAMILY MEMBERS, AND FRIENDS

As a family member or close friend of a returning veteran, even though you didn't experience the dangers of war yourself, you're probably discovering that you too are deeply affected by your veteran's experience. Here are some common problems that impact family members and close friends of returning veterans.

Nightmares, Flashbacks, and Disturbing Images of Posttraumatic Stress

Many veterans of Iraq and Afghanistan return home with symptoms of posttraumatic stress such as nightmares, flashbacks, or unwanted memories of war that cause them to feel different from others. They may wonder whether anyone can understand what they experienced. Their thoughts and memories about their war experience can be so powerful that you may believe your veteran is no longer interested in being part of the family. Yet they may fear that if they share what they went through, you'll be as disturbed as they are. Like your veteran, you may have poor sleep and disturbing dreams even without knowing the details of his or her experience.

Avoidance Symptoms of Posttraumatic Stress

Avoidance, a common problem for returning veterans, can be one of the most challenging symptoms for family and close friends to deal with. Withdrawing can be a way to "protect" themselves from the fear of losing their family, but to family members it may feel like rejection, not love. Unfortunately, when you feel rejected you're likely to avoid direct conversations about the problem. This can leave your veteran feeling excluded from family matters and worsen his or her insecurities or bad self-image. If he or she is not interested in going out, you may become isolated too. Losing your social supports can make you depressed, anxious, or even physically ill.

Arousal Symptoms of Posttraumatic Stress

Arousal symptoms can lead a returning veteran to be on guard, overly alert, and quickly enraged. He or she may see danger for family members everywhere, leading them to impose new restrictions and rules to make sure he or she always knows where family members are. Some things you and your family enjoyed before suddenly become "unacceptable" or "irresponsible," causing more problems. And your veteran's "short fuse" may make you feel like you're walking on eggshells.

"Contagious" Arousal

If a person's physical arousal (heart rate, blood pressure, and sweating) increases during a disagreement with a spouse, the partner's physical arousal also increases. When your partner has gone through a wartime experience and has problems with increased arousal, you can become "stressed out" too, and it's even possible for the arousal to spread to your whole family. Couples and families may quickly "go from zero to 60" when discussing emotion-charged topics. Your family may also become more sensitive to potential threats outside the family, anticipating that something bad will happen to a family member.

Depression

If your veteran is depressed, it can leave you feeling rejected and unloved. He or she may lose interest in family activities formerly enjoyed, including celebrations, family dinners, even sex. Negative thinking that comes with your veteran's depression can make you feel like a "dark cloud" is hanging over your home or your friendship. Your future may seem as bleak as your veteran portrays it. You've tried all sorts of ways to "cheer" your veteran up—cooking his or her favorite meal, watching his or her favorite movie, or surprising him or her with tickets to a baseball game or a concert. But now you may have decided to just leave him or her alone and go about your family activities. Yet this can only make you and your veteran feel *more* negative and depressed.

Alcohol or Drug Use

Your veteran's drug or alcohol use can impact you too. It can create distance from you and feel much the same as if he or she were having a love affair with another person. Then you may begin to withdraw from your veteran, too, not involving him or her in decisions because you feel you cannot trust your veteran's judgment. Your veteran may become less responsible, spending money that the family doesn't have on his or her addiction. Children may get into trouble to try to distract him or her away from the drugs or alcohol. Or your veteran's mood may take over the entire family and lead everyone to be very careful around him or her. Your veteran may even become physically or verbally abusive. Ignoring your veteran can reenforce the drinking or drug use. If you try to protect your veteran from dealing with his or her use of alcohol or drugs and the underlying war-zone issues, you only encourage continued use. You can end up feeling angry, depressed, helpless, or disappointed as a result of your veteran's alcohol or drug problems.

2

Strengthening Your Mind and Body

Veterans returning from Iraq and Afghanistan often show amazing courage and survival skills, not only in war but also at home. Consider Mark, for example,

> **Mark**, who sustained a gunshot wound to his shoulder in Iraq, has returned to his home in Humboldt, California, where he is studying to take the law school admission test. Although he can no longer lift weights the way he used to, he has changed his workout routine and goes to either the gym or physical therapy at least three times a week. He's spending lots of time getting to know his one-year-old son, who was born while he was deployed, and renewing his relationship with his wife, Gina, as a way to focus more on the present than the past. Since his return, he has worked hard to develop a small website design business. His attention to the business and the law school test helps keep him from watching too much news about Iraq or thinking too often about his war experience.
>
> Another veteran, **Donna**, who served back-to-back tours, first in Afghanistan and then in Iraq, has returned to her job as a car mechanic in Spokane, Washington. Her experience at war affected her deeply and made her think seriously about what she is doing in her life. Although she was drinking wine most nights to fall asleep when she first returned, she decided to quit because she thought about the bad effects on her health. Instead, she's doing yoga and meditation before she sleeps. She

also decided to enroll in college part-time to earn her
bachelor's degree in fine arts, using her talents in drawing and
painting. She attends group therapy once a week at the VA
Medical Center and volunteers at the local museum to help with
her readjustment to civilian life.

This chapter will give you practical tools to bolster the courage
and survival skills you already possess for coping with the aftereffects of war and the pressures of readjusting to civilian life. For
weeks, months, perhaps even years, you'll think back on your
war experiences and remember both positive and negative memories. As you go through your day-to-day life, thoughts, images, and
memories of things that happened while you were deployed will
flash through your mind. At these moments, you may feel like you
should have done some things differently. You may beat yourself
up inside, thinking that you didn't do the best job possible.

This chapter will reinforce the survival skills and strengths
you already have to help you combat war-related stress. It will
also give you an overview of relaxation "drills" to help reduce
your anxiety as you readjust stateside. And it will review techniques you can use for taking "stronger" care of yourself, including tips for sleep, exercise, and healthy eating. Although you have
been inundated with information about healthy coping at military debriefings, use this collection of coping strategies as you
would a handy toolbox. Pick a tool whenever you need it to help
with your transition back to civilian life. It will make your journey home from war less bumpy.

A Strengths-Oriented Approach

You already have a set of survival skills and strengths—positive
qualities and abilities you bring to tough situations—to help you
persevere and thrive. They helped you survive the war. Don't
neglect to use these strengths on your return.

Now, when faced with difficult situations, you might be focusing on what's going wrong in your life, instead of what's going right. But if you only focus on what's going wrong, two things happen:

- You let your problems have more power over your life than they should.
- You "forget" or minimize the abilities you have to deal with hardships.

Remember, you survived the war and the separation from your family and friends. You also dealt with difficult situations in your life before deployment. If you apply your survival skills and strengths, you can face difficult situations at home as courageously as you did at war.

Do the three exercises below. They will help you rediscover your strengths.

EXERCISE #1

Make a list of challenging experiences you overcame in your life before going to war, such as the death of a family member or friend, finding a new job, going through a divorce, moving to a new city as a child, overcoming an illness, surviving an accident, or sustaining a financial blow. Your list and the questions that follow can help remind you of your strengths and abilities to face any problem you may be experiencing now. This is not a time to think about what you didn't do in past difficult situations but to focus on what you *did* do well at these times.

After making this list, choose from it one situation you think you handled especially well and answer the following questions:

   ❑ What did you do that helped you handle this situation?
   ❑ Did surviving this situation change your view of yourself? If yes, how?
   ❑ Were you surprised at your abilities? Why or why not?

❐ Are there others in your life who would not have
been surprised at your abilities? If yes, what do they
know about you that would lead them to feel that
way?

❐ What specific qualities do you have that helped you
handle this difficult situation?

If possible, review these answers with your partner, family
member, or friend. Listen to any additional ideas they have about
what they see as your strengths in dealing with tough situations.

EXERCISE #2

Make a list of difficult situations you overcame during the war.
Examples might be living through a mortar blast, making it
through a blocked highway while under fire, saving a buddy from
injury, running a successful mission, retrieving a broken vehicle
during a turbulent convoy, or sleeping in your truck for months
on end during the awful heat. Again, never mind what you may
not have done so well during these situations. Focus on what you
did do effectively. Then choose from the list one of the situations
you feel you handled especially well, and answer the following
questions:

❐ What did you do that helped you handle this war
situation?

❐ Did surviving this situation change your view of
yourself? If yes, how?

❐ Were you surprised at your abilities? Why or why
not?

❐ Are there others in your life who would not have
been surprised at your abilities? If yes, what do they
know about you that would lead them to feel that
way?

❐ What specific qualities do you have that helped you
handle this difficult wartime situation?

If you can, review these answers with your partner, family
member, or friend. Take in any ideas they may propose about what
they see as your strengths in dealing with wartime situations.

After completing these two exercises, make a list of three sur-vival skills or strengths you possess and have used during chal-lenging situations both before and during the war. Hold on to this list and read it when you're faced with postdeployment problems. This list will remind you that you already come prepared to face life's problems!

EXERCISE #3

Some challenging experiences of war also are interspersed with moments of satisfaction, thrill, or humor. You might laugh at some comical aspect of an operation—a few seconds of black humor that broke up the monotony of the day. You might recall living through a situation that was bizarre, absurd, or surreal. To fully integrate your war experiences, spend time reviewing the humor-ous or enjoyable moments you had while deployed. Record at least two events that you felt were funny, absurd, or lighthearted. Write them down, or use a video or audiotape. Hold on to these stories and, if you can, share them with family and friends to remind you of the positive memories of your time overseas.

Relaxation Drills

Besides focusing on your strengths and remembering positive moments overseas, you'll need to learn to achieve a state of relax-ation as the cornerstone to reducing anxiety and stress from your war experience. Relaxation drills are more than engaging in "relaxing" activities such as reading, hiking, watching television, or enjoying a sunset.

Relaxation drills reverse the "fight-or-flight response." As you'll recall from Chapter 1, the fight-or-flight response can be protective because it activates the body like an alarm system to avoid harm when there's a threat of danger. But this reaction tends to remain on overdrive even after you've returned from war. As a consequence, your body and mind may feel on high alert even when there's no real danger.

In 1975, Dr. Herbert Benson coined the term "relaxation response" to describe a specific physical state that helps overturn the fight-or-flight response and turn down the alarm system when you feel on high alert for no obvious reason. When the relaxation response kicks in, changes take place in your body that lessen anxiety and tension. Your heart and breathing rates go down. Your blood pressure decreases. Your muscles become less tense. When your body slows down, your mind quiets down too. As your body and mind become calm, you feel more in control.

One way to combat anxiety and stress is to learn, practice, and use exercises that tap into this relaxation response. The following four relaxation drills—Smooth Breathing, Imagining Safety, Muscle Relaxation, and Simple Outlets—will help train your mind and body to achieve this relaxation response.

The key to learning these relaxation drills is to practice them every day, as you would a new sports technique. After doing them regularly for several weeks, the payoff will be substantial: You'll begin to feel more relaxed for longer periods of time.

What's so convenient about these relaxation drills is that you carry them with you wherever you go. Once you become good at them, you can use them almost anywhere, anytime you feel yourself becoming stressed or anxious.

SMOOTH BREATHING

One of the simplest and most effective relaxation drills is called *Smooth Breathing.* Often when you're feeling anxious or stressed, you "overbreathe" or hyperventilate. You breathe in too much oxygen and breathe out too much carbon dioxide. Then your blood vessels constrict and you can't use the oxygen appropriately, so you may feel sensations of dizziness, lightheadedness, tingling, and numbness in your hands and feet, flushing in your face, and muscle tightness. Here's how to combat these reactions:

1. Select a quiet place where you won't be disturbed.

2. Sit or lie comfortably.

3. Rate your level of anxiety on a scale of 0 to 10, where 0 is feeling totally calm and 10 is feeling extremely anxious. Use the Anxiety Rating Scale in the box at the end of this drill.

4. Take a few seconds to focus.

5. Place one hand on your stomach and the other on your chest. You want your breathing to come from deep down in your stomach, not from your chest.

6. Inhale slowly through your nose and expand your stomach as much as possible.

7. As you inhale, picture your stomach filling with air while you say the number "1" silently to yourself.

8. Use the hand you have placed on your stomach to feel that you're breathing smoothly, easily, and deeply from your stomach, not from your chest; don't take big, deep gulps of breath.

9. Then exhale. When you do this, let the air move gradually out from your nose; you don't want to release all the air suddenly. Extend the exhalation for as long as you can.

10. As you exhale, picture your stomach deflating while saying the word "Relax" silently to yourself.

11. Repeat this process. That is, think of the number 2 as you inhale, and of the word Relax as you exhale. Continue this pattern until you reach 30, focusing on the number when you inhale and the word Relax when you exhale. Then start counting backward down to 1.

12. Again, rate your level of anxiety on a scale of 0 to 10, where 0 is feeling totally calm and 10 is feeling extremely anxious. Use the Anxiety Rating Scale on the next page.

13. As you concentrate on the numbers and words, don't be concerned if your mind wanders or other thoughts intrude. Just let these thoughts pass through your mind like floating clouds, then refocus your attention on the numbers and words.

Practice this drill at a regularly scheduled time twice a day, for at least 10 minutes each time, and for at least one week until you become good at it.

In a journal or notebook, keep track of when you practice this drill by recording the date and time, as noted in the Anxiety Rating Chart below. Over time, you should notice a reduction in your anxiety ratings.

ANXIETY RATING SCALE										
0	1	2	3	4	5	6	7	8	9	10
Relaxed								Extremely Anxious		

ANXIETY RATING CHART
Date:
Time Started:
Time Finished:
Anxiety Level Before:
Anxiety Level After:

IMAGINING SAFETY

Another popular relaxation drill that can be used to combat anxiety and stress related to your war experience is called *Imagining Safety*. After returning from war, you may carry some distressing or frightening mental images from your extraordinary experiences. These images can be powerful and overwhelming. They can create fear, anxiety, anger, or other strong emotions and impact how you behave. But, similarly, a positive image of a safe place can produce a relaxation response that will help create a sense of calmness and control. This is sometimes referred to as "going to a happy place inside your mind." Even if you've tried this exercise before and found that it didn't work or was difficult to do, give it another chance. It works for many veterans after they try it a few times. For some, *Imagining Safety* is the most helpful relaxation strategy in their coping toolbox.

Imagining Safety involves purposefully visualizing a mental image of a peaceful scene to help reduce your war-tied anxiety and stress. Think of this drill as if you were taking a mini-vacation. Picture a favorite relaxing scene—a safe place that brings you comfort and peace. It may be a mountain, a forest, a beach, a ranch, a park, a stream, or any image you associate with calmness, security, and comfort. If at first you can't come up with your own relaxing scene, try the one below. Focus on this scene by specifically noticing how it affects each of your senses—what you see, hear, touch, taste, and smell. Also pay attention to the emotions you feel and the thoughts you have when you imagine this scene.

When you first learn this drill, you may want to read the following script aloud (or write a similar one yourself about a favorite relaxing place), or ask someone else to and tape record it. Decide whether you want to use your voice or whether you'd be more relaxed listening to someone else's voice. Then follow these steps:

1. Select a comfortable position on a chair or bed in a quiet place.

2. Rate your level of anxiety on a scale of 0 to 10, where 0 is feeling totally calm and 10 is feeling extremely anxious. Use the Anxiety Rating Scale on page 41.

3. Take a few moments to become calm.

4. Close your eyes after you've become comfortable and calm.

5. Now play the tape to help you picture in your mind this beach scene or the relaxing scene you've selected, paying close attention to the sights, sounds, smells, tastes, feelings, emotions, and thoughts evoked by the image. This drill will take about 5 to 10 minutes to complete.

SCRIPT: A DAY AT THE BEACH

While walking along a white sandy beach, you're pleasantly surprised by how few people are here to witness the sheer natural beauty of this serene place.

You notice a rainbow sun-umbrella off to the right with two turquoise beach towels under it. And off to the left, a small boy is flying a bright yellow kite and laughing.

Immediately in front of you, a pristine white seashell catches your eye. It is small and delicate. You pick it up and stare at its dainty edges, then set it gently back on the sand.

Ahead of you in the distance, the water glistens in many shades of green and blue. Small ripples grace the beach, as the water ebbs and flows smoothly. You hear the soothing sounds of the waves.

In the far distance, a sailboat glides peacefully. It barely looks like it's moving. Its white sail shimmers and billows in the breeze.

When you approach the water, you feel the soft moist sand under your feet, taste the salty spray in the air, and feel a chill as the water brushes over your ankles and feet. You're surprised at how fresh and vibrant the water feels on your skin.

When you glance up, you realize that the sky has never looked bluer than today. A few white clouds roll off in the distance, plump and lofty. You hear the sounds of seagulls flying over you, and wonder where they're going.

You decide to take your sleek yellow raft into the water for a leisurely float. When you position your body on this raft comfortably as you make your way out into the water, the sun beams down warmly on your face, shoulders, and arms, soaking through your skin. You hear the water ripple back and forth. You touch the surf with your right hand as you float along on your raft. Everything around you says "calmness," and you're becoming more relaxed.

You look farther out and see another sailboat. Moving slowly and gracefully, this sailboat's blue-and-white striped sail catches your eye. You feel rested and at peace as you continue to float freely.

You notice a lighthouse way off in the distance. You feel relieved and reassured, knowing that if you were to become lost at sea, this beautiful white lighthouse would be your guide forever. Its sole purpose is to keep you safe. On seeing this lighthouse, you let go more and more, relaxing deeper and deeper as you float along the soft waves on your smooth raft.

This is your day of relaxation. You have no worries. They have been left at home. When you hear the comforting sounds of the surf, you feel restful and calm.

Now and then a light breeze touches your cheeks, refreshing and invigorating your body. You're becoming more and more content.

The sun warmly caresses your body and your soul as you drift here and there on your raft, wherever the gentle waves take you. You feel still and quiet. There are no concerns or distractions, only a sense of simplicity, peace, and tranquility.

You fall deeper into a state of relaxation. Your mind and body feel in harmony with this wonderful ocean, so vast and pure.

In a few moments you'll begin to return to an alert, wakeful state of mind. This will occur gradually, as you slowly count from 1 to 10, so that when you reach 10 you'll be fully awake, and you will open your eyes. At 10, you feel fully refreshed and alert.

Now, rate your level of anxiety on a scale of 0 to 10, where 0 is feeling totally calm and 10 is feeling extremely anxious. Use the Anxiety Rating Scale on page 41.

Practice this drill at a regularly scheduled time, at least once a day, and for at least one week until you become good at it.

In a journal or notebook, keep track of when you practice this drill by recording the date and time, as noted in the Anxiety Rating Chart on page 41. Over time, you should notice a reduction in your anxiety ratings.

MUSCLE RELAXATION

Another useful relaxation drill is called *Muscle Relaxation*. This exercise is especially helpful for reducing muscle tension and worry. It involves tensing different sets of muscles in your body and then relaxing them. The goal is to become aware of the difference between tension and calmness in your body. This drill will help you learn first to detect tension in your body and then to reduce anxiety before it rises to higher levels.

Read the following script aloud, or ask someone else to do it and tape record it. Decide whether you want to use your voice or whether you'd be more relaxed listening to someone else's voice on the recording. Then play the tape to guide you through the drill.

While listening to the tape, envision a state of relaxation spreading throughout your body, step-by-step, from your feet up through your stomach, your chest, and finally to your face. This drill will take about 20 to 30 minutes to complete. For each muscle group, first focus for 10 seconds in a tensed state, then focus for 20 seconds in a relaxed state.

1. Get into a comfortable sitting position where your head leans back against a wall. You can choose to close your eyes or to keep them open, whichever is most comfortable for you.

2. Rate your level of anxiety on a scale of 0 to 10, where 0 is feeling totally calm and 10 is feeling extremely anxious. Use the Anxiety Rating Scale on page 41.

3. Take a few moments to get focused.

4. First, focus on your breathing. Make sure it's slow and smooth. Breathe in smoothly and say, "1." Breathe out easily and say, "Relax." Focus on your breaths. Breathe in and say, "2." Breathe out and say, "Relax." Continue this smooth and easy breathing. Feel the cool air as you breathe in and the warm air as you breathe out.

5. Now focus on the muscles in your lower legs and feet. Concentrate intensely on this set of muscles for a few moments. Now build tension in your lower legs by flexing your feet and pulling your toes up toward the ceiling. Hold this position for 10 seconds. Feel the tightness and tension spreading throughout your toes, feet, ankles, shins, and calves. After 10 seconds, release the tension by deflexing your feet and letting your legs relax comfortably onto the chair. Focus on the difference between the state of tension you felt when you flexed and the state of relaxation now moving through your feet and lower legs. Enjoy the sense of warmth, heaviness, and comfort spreading through your feet and lower legs, for 20 seconds.

6. Next move to your upper legs. Concentrate intensely on the muscles in your upper legs for a few moments. Now build tension in your upper legs by pulling your knees together and lifting your legs off the chair or couch. Hold this position for 10 seconds. Feel the tightness and tension spreading through your upper legs. After 10 seconds, release the tension by letting your legs drop down onto the chair. Focus on the difference between the state of tension you felt while flexing and the state of relaxation now moving through your upper legs. Enjoy the sense of warmth, heaviness, and comfort spreading through your upper legs, for 20 seconds.

7. Continue to move up your body, to the muscles in your stomach and chest. Concentrate intensely on this muscle group for a few moments. Now build tension in your stomach and chest by taking in a deep breath and holding it as you pull your stomach toward your spine. Hold this position for 10 seconds. Feel the tightness and tension spreading throughout your stomach and chest. After 10 seconds, let go

of the tension by releasing your stomach. Focus on the difference between the state of tension you felt and the state of relaxation now filling your stomach and chest. Enjoy the sense of warmth, heaviness, and comfort spreading throughout your stomach and chest, for 20 seconds.

8. Now move to the muscles in your shoulders. Concentrate intensely on the muscles in this area for a few moments. Now build tension in your shoulders by pulling them up as close to your ears as you can. Hold this position for 10 seconds. Feel the tightness and tension spreading through your shoulders. After 10 seconds, release the tension by dropping your shoulders down and letting them droop comfortably. Focus on the difference between the state of tension and the state of relaxation now moving through your shoulders. Enjoy the sense of warmth, heaviness, and comfort spreading through your shoulders, for 20 seconds.

9. Next move your attention to your hands and arms. Concentrate intensely on the muscles in your hands and arms for a few moments. Build tension in your hands and arms by making fists with both your hands. Bend your wrists up to pull your fists up. Hold this position for 10 seconds. Feel the tightness and tension spreading through your hands and arms. Now release the tension by letting go of your fists and unbending your wrists. Focus on the difference between the state of tension and the state of relaxation emerging in your hands and arms. Enjoy the sense of warmth, heaviness, and comfort spreading through your hands and arms, for 20 seconds.

10. A sense of relaxation is spreading more and more throughout various muscles in your body. Let's move on to the muscles in your neck. Concentrate intensely on those muscles for a few moments. Build tension in your neck by pulling your chin down toward your chest as far as you can. Hold this position for 10 seconds. Feel the tightness and tension spreading through your neck. After 10 seconds, release the tension and let your head rest against the wall. Focus on the difference between the state of tension and the state of

relaxation emerging in your neck. Enjoy the sense of warmth, heaviness, and comfort spreading through your neck, for 20 seconds.

11. Now focus on different parts of your face. First, attend to your mouth and jaw, concentrating intensely on those muscles for a few moments. Build tension by clenching your teeth tightly together for 10 seconds. Feel the tightness and tension spreading through your mouth and jaw. After 10 seconds, release the tension, unclenching your teeth and letting your mouth and jaw drop. Focus on the difference between the state of tension and the state of relaxation now moving in your mouth and jaw. Enjoy the sense of warmth, heaviness, and comfort spreading through your mouth and jaw, for 20 seconds.

12. As a state of relaxation spreads around your face, focus on your eyes. Concentrate intensely on the muscles around and behind your eyes for a few moments. Build tension in your eyes by squeezing them tightly together. Hold this position for 10 seconds. Feel the tightness and tension spreading through your eyes. After 10 seconds, release the tension by relaxing your eye muscles. Focus on the difference between the state of tension and the state of relaxation now moving around and behind your eyes. Enjoy the sense of warmth, heaviness, and comfort spreading through your eyes, for 20 seconds.

13. Continue to relax the muscles in your face by focusing on your upper forehead. Concentrate intensely on those muscles for a few moments. Build tension in your upper forehead by raising your eyebrows up as high as possible. Hold this position for 10 seconds. Feel the tightness and tension spreading throughout your upper forehead. After 10 seconds, release the tension by letting your eyebrows down. Focus on the difference between the state of tension and the state of relaxation now moving in your upper forehead. Enjoy the sense of warmth, heaviness, and comfort spreading through your forehead, for 20 seconds.

14. At this point, relaxation has spread throughout your whole body. Starting with your feet and legs, relaxation then moved to your stomach and chest. Next the relaxation spread into your hands and arms, then to your neck, and to your face. Let your whole body become more and more relaxed. Let *all* the tension leave your body. If you feel remaining tension in any muscle, envision it floating away. Sink deeper and deeper into a state of peace and warmth, with relaxation deepening further and further throughout your body. Feel heaviness and comfort filling each of your muscle groups more and more. Enjoy this state of deep relaxation. Continue to focus on your breathing. Make sure it's slow and smooth. Feel the cool air as you breathe in and the warm air as you breathe out.

15. Now, counting from 1 to 10, you will gradually become more awake and alert. When you reach the number 10, sit up and open your eyes into a wakeful, alert state.

16. Now, rate your level of anxiety on a scale of 0 to 10, where 0 is feeling totally calm and 10 is feeling extremely anxious. Use the Anxiety Rating Scale on page 41.

17. Having completed this exercise, reflect on how it was for you to do this muscle relaxation procedure:

- Were there any particular muscle groups that were hard for you to relax?
- Do you feel more relaxed after this exercise than before?
- Did you find it hard to concentrate on certain sets of muscles?

Practice this drill at regularly scheduled times, at least once a day, for at least one week, using the tape to guide you until you get good at it.

In a journal or notebook, keep track of when you practice this drill by recording the date and time, as noted in the Anxiety Rating Chart on page 41. Over time, you should notice a reduction in your anxiety ratings.

SIMPLE OUTLETS

Another useful relaxation drill is to find greater happiness and peace in your life through *Simple Outlets*. This strategy involves engaging in small but meaningful acts that focus your attention away from war memories and distress, toward pleasant, relaxing things you see, hear, smell, taste, touch, or think about in your immediate environment. Ask yourself how you can take charge of and create more calmness in your present situation by involving different senses that make you feel positive. Use the examples below as a guide:

Sight: What can I look at that will make me feel more at peace at this moment?

Examples: A painting, birds, the sky, stars, the beach, a fire, a photo of a loved one.

Hearing: What can I listen to that will make me feel more at peace at this moment?

Examples: Relaxing music, sounds from nature (waves, birds, a waterfall, rain, the wind), a fountain.

Smell: What can I smell that will make me feel more at peace at this moment?

Examples: Incense, perfume, cologne, spices, a scented candle, flowers, home cooking, a pie in the oven.

Taste: What can I taste that will make me feel more at peace at this moment?

Examples: A special meal, a delicious dessert, a favorite candy, a refreshing fruit smoothie drink.

Touch: What can I touch that will make me feel more at peace at this moment?

> Examples: A hot shower or bubble bath, a
> furry pet, a comfortable couch, a smooth
> rock.

Thoughts: What can I think about that will make me feel more at peace at this moment?

> Examples: "I am safe, now that I am
> home"; "I did my best in the service of my
> country"; "I can trust that over time I will
> adjust to life back home"; "I'm a decent,
> kind person going through a difficult time.
> I will get better."

In a journal or notebook, keep track of what simple outlets bring you a sense of peace and relaxation, then incorporate them into your daily routine.

HIGHLIGHTS OF RELAXATION DRILLS

At the beginning of your training, remember to practice the four relaxation drills described in this chapter when you're *not* anxious. After you become proficient, use them whenever you're feeling moderate to high anxiety levels, to help reduce your stress.

Recognize that progress will be slow and modest at first, but the more you practice and use these drills, the better the results will be over time. You'll gradually be able to achieve greater periods of relaxation in your life.

Discover which of the relaxation drills work best for you or fit your style most comfortably. Use them often.

Taking "Stronger" Care of Yourself

After fighting in a war, you'll need to spend extra time rallying your strength to fortify yourself for your adjustment to the home front. This section describes a handful of ways to take "stronger" care of yourself, including strategies for improving sleep, exercise, and eating habits. These strategies complement the strengths you already possess and the relaxation drills you just learned, making you better able to combat anxiety and stress.

Taking good care of yourself means having the courage to treat yourself with honor, pride, and importance—as you would a fellow veteran. By taking good care of yourself, you'll achieve greater balance, stability, and peace in your postdeployment life.

Focusing on your own needs can be a difficult transition to make, because in military service you're not used to putting yourself first. You're trained to be loyal to your buddies and to follow orders for the war mission. And after seeing the chaos of war, you may now feel that nothing really matters anymore—therefore, *you* don't really matter. Or you may think you don't deserve happiness because others didn't make it home at all. But now that you're home, your "mission" has changed, and it's up to you to make your life matter. Taking care of yourself is an essential component of making the most of your life—for yourself and for the important people in your life.

Taking care of yourself is often confused with being self-centered or selfish, but this is far from the truth. In fact, caring and finding time for yourself frees you to give more to others because it strengthens and revitalizes you. Making yourself #1 also means limiting or stopping unhealthy activities that compound your stress.

TAKE A NEWS HOLIDAY

You may feel compelled to watch the news, read the morning paper, listen to radio programming, or surf the Internet for information about the current conflicts in Iraq and Afghanistan. Having been at war, you want to learn how your fellow military service members are doing. You want to keep up with the action on a day-to-day basis. Ready access to the Internet makes it easier than ever to have such news at your fingertips and to actually communicate with those who are still deployed.

But these war-related news activities don't help you adjust to being home. Instead, they invite you to relive your war experiences and to stay immersed in that period of your life. This continuous engagement in war, even though long-distance, makes it harder to reconnect with your family, friends, and community stateside. Information about the current wars from newspapers, the Internet, television, radio, movies, telephone calls, e-mail, or written correspondence with military service members who are still deployed is likely to trigger strong physical and emotional reactions within you. These reactions, which may happen almost automatically, can increase your overall stress level and set off disturbing memories of experiences you had while deployed.

As gripping as it is to follow what's going on in these conflicts, you're better off limiting the amount of news you take in about OIF and OEF. Better yet, stop following war news altogether for a time. Instead, pick up old hobbies you didn't have the chance to do while you were deployed. Watch relaxing or funny television shows. Read mystery novels or interesting books. Flip through magazines or dabble in cooking. Play sports with your children or friends or go to a new exhibition at a museum.

Participating in activities unrelated to the war will fortify your resources and energy so you can focus more on readjusting to life at home. If you find it too difficult to completely stop following war news, at least stop watching the news on television and get your information about the war from newspapers or a weekly news magazine. It's much easier to put a newspaper down or skip stories that trigger anxiety than it is to control the bombardment of visual images and death notices from television.

REVISIT OLD HOBBIES

Think about nonmilitary things you really enjoy. Ask yourself why you don't allow yourself to do these things more often. You may discover, for example, that you don't let yourself enjoy certain things because you aren't used to giving to yourself, or maybe you think you don't need or deserve nice things. For example, you might enjoy having some nice new accessory for your car or buying some CDs, but you deny yourself the pleasure of these "extras." Or you might like an activity such as photography, woodworking, going to the beach, or working out at the gym, but you don't make time for it because you feel you'd be shirking your family or work responsibilities.

Taking stronger care of yourself means breaking the habit of saying "no" to yourself. Instead, let yourself savor some well-deserved treats, downtime, or fun activities, and you'll find that you can cope better with civilian life and both help and enjoy those around you.

One helpful way to think about taking stronger care of yourself is to categorize the actions or things you do for yourself according to the different dimensions of your life. Consider the following, for instance.

PHYSICAL

Examples: Going to doctors' appointments, eating a healthy diet, exercising regularly, taking prescribed medications as directed, getting proper sleep.

EMOTIONAL

Examples: Writing in a journal, doing artwork, listening to music, spending time with family or friends, playing with pets, gardening.

INTELLECTUAL

Examples: Reading, taking a class, discussing an intellectually challenging topic with family or friends, learning a new hobby or skill, watching intellectually stimulating television shows or movies.

SPIRITUAL

Examples: Doing meditation, volunteering in the community, making charity donations, participating in a spiritual organization, attending religious services, reflecting on what's important in your life.

PROFESSIONAL

Examples: Asking your boss for a work schedule that fits best with your family life, taking small breaks during your workday, leaving work on time (not staying late or overworking), arranging your work environment so it's comfortable and feels safe, taking a training class, considering a job change if you're dissatisfied.

SLEEP BETTER

Taking stronger care of yourself in terms of the physical dimension of your life includes getting good sleep. Sleep problems are extremely common among veterans who have returned from war. While deployed, you couldn't get the regular sleep that you were probably used to before the war. Constant mortar attacks, bare living environments such as sleeping in a truck or tent, and other disturbances made it hard to fall and stay asleep. Carrying out military duties 24/7, you may have only been able to sleep a few hours here and there. In fact, at certain times during the war, you may not have slept for several days and nights in a row, depending on the threat or crisis at that moment. And when you *could* lie down to sleep, you probably were on high alert in anticipation of the enemy's next attack. It might have been essential to remain vigilant at night to protect yourself and your buddies from danger. Even when you were finally able to shut your eyes and sleep, before you knew it you had to rise early for duty.

Nightmares often develop from combat experiences. They may have started while you were deployed, and still persist. Or they may have begun once you got back home. Regardless of when they started, your nightmares are probably directly or indirectly related to your wartime activities. Often, they contain themes of death, helplessness, fear, escape, gore, revenge, or other war imagery. They can be terrifying, confusing, and disturbing.

The many sleep changes you faced for months on end while deployed have impacted the regular rhythm of your sleep or your "body clock." Now that you're home, it's no wonder you continue to have trouble sleeping—difficulty or fear of falling asleep, getting only a few broken hours of sleep, waking earlier than you intended, or oversleeping. Veterans commonly complain of the following sleep problems:

- *I can't fall asleep.*
- *I wake on and off throughout the night.*
- *I wake up much earlier than I would like to.*
- *I sleep too much.*
- *I'm afraid to fall asleep, so I stay up most of the night.*
- *I wake up covered in sweat. I end up having to change my sleepwear and the sheets.*
- *I have nightmares that wake me up.*
- *I fall asleep during the day because I'm so exhausted.*
- *I can only fall asleep with the television on.*
- *I've become an insomniac since being at war.*
- *My partner no longer sleeps with me because of the commotion I cause during sleep.*
- *The crazy things I do in my sleep frighten my partner.*

If you have these kinds of sleep problems, you aren't alone. Unfortunately, not getting enough sleep has many negative effects on your mind and body. For instance, sleep deprivation can make you more edgy, moody, and angry; less active and social; more depressed; and less able to fight off colds and infections. Lack of sleep can lessen your productivity at work and at home because you have trouble concentrating, paying attention, and accomplishing complex tasks. Functioning without adequate sleep is like fighting a war without body armor. You're more prone to "attacks" and "mistakes," like snapping at your partner for no good reason, forgetting things that you normally would remember, and struggling to do work projects or household chores.

There's no doubt about it: Getting proper sleep is essential for maintaining your physical and emotional well-being. It also is crucial for staying active in family, work, school, and social activities. The goal is to get close to eight hours of restful sleep each night. Below are tips for improving your sleep.

SLEEP TIPS: 19 WAYS TO GET BETTER ZZZZS

1. **Maintain a regular sleep schedule.** Go to sleep and wake up at the same times every day, even on weekends.

2. **Make your bedroom or sleep environment as comfortable as possible.** Create a comfortable room temperature; make sure your bedroom is dark enough; invest in pillows, bedding, and a mattress that are relaxing for you; and make your environment noise-free.

3. **Use your bed only for sleep and sex, not for other activities.** Don't use your bed for paying bills, working on your laptop, watching television, eating, looking at paperwork, or studying. Your bed should be associated in your mind with two pleasurable activities—sleep and sex.

4. **Establish a "wind down" routine before you go to bed.** Use a routine to relax and prepare your mind and body for rest. You may want to do one of the relaxation drills described earlier, such as *Imagining Safety*, or read a good book, listen to calm music, take a warm bath, or light a scented candle. This "wind-down" period should not include watching or reading war-related news or other material that will get you stirred up.

5. **Don't consume drinks or food with caffeine (for example, coffee, sodas, tea, and chocolate) within six hours of your bedtime.** Caffeine, a stimulant, will rev your body up and keep you from falling asleep. If you want to have a bever-

age before bedtime, try something like an herbal tea or hot milk, which can have a sedative effect. But make sure you don't drink too much of any liquid before going to sleep.

6. **Don't use alcohol or illicit drugs to help you fall asleep.** Although using alcohol or certain illicit drugs may make you fall asleep by numbing your feelings or blotting out your nightmares, ultimately these substances disturb your regular sleep patterns and can feed depression. If you drink alcohol at dinnertime, limit yourself to one drink.

7. **Avoid regular or extended use of over-the-counter or physician-prescribed sleep aids.** Although these medications may help you get to sleep, they're no long-term solution. They can cause unwanted side effects such as morning grogginess. What's more, regular use of sleep aids will prevent you from reestablishing your natural sleep cycle and can quickly lead to dependency.

8. **Exercise regularly.** A regular exercise routine is very helpful for reducing insomnia, stress, and anxiety. But don't exercise at night, within three hours of your bedtime—it can rev your body up.

9. **Stay active.** During the day, keep your mind and body active by participating in hobbies or stimulating tasks. Research shows that active, motivated people sleep better, while less-active, sedentary people don't sleep as well.

10. **Don't eat heavy food before you go to bed.** Stay away from foods that can lead to indigestion or heartburn. If you're hungry at bedtime, eat a light snack high in carbohydrates and low in protein. Eating at regularly scheduled mealtimes during the day can also help to reestablish a normal sleep/wake cycle.

11. **Quit smoking or using chewing tobacco.** Nicotine, like caffeine, is a stimulant that will interfere with sleep.

12. **Avoid or limit naps during the day.** It's easy to resort to napping in the daytime if you have trouble sleeping at night. But napping during the day often makes it harder to fall asleep at night. If you do choose to take a nap during the day, limit it to about 30 minutes, and don't nap late in the afternoon.

13. **Stop watching the clock.** Don't watch the clock as you try to fall asleep. And don't keep checking the clock if you wake up during sleep. Clock-watching will make you more anxious and upset about not sleeping. Then you become more aroused and can't sleep.

14. **Get up if you can't sleep.** If you can't fall asleep after about 20 to 30 minutes, or if you wake up during the night and can't fall back to sleep, get up, go to another room, find a comfortable couch or chair, and engage in a low-key, relaxing activity such as listening to soothing music, reading a light book, or flipping through a magazine. Return to bed when you become sleepy. You may have to repeat this pattern several times if you keep waking. Eventually, though, by sticking with this routine you'll retrain your body to sleep when you're in bed.

15. **Try not to worry.** If you begin worrying at bedtime about things you need to do tomorrow, something that happened earlier in the day, events that occurred while you were deployed, or other concerns—which is very common—try to refocus your mind on something else that's pleasant or neutral. Do the breathing exercise described earlier in this chapter, or listen to relaxing music. Turning off your worries as you go to sleep can be very hard. If you feel you need "worry time," set aside a period earlier in the day when you can dwell on things you're concerned about, and write them down. When you go to bed, tell yourself that you have your "worry list" ready for tomorrow, and see if this helps.

16. **Make sleep a top priority.** Valuing good sleep is just as important as other priorities in your life. It may require developing a work schedule that allows for regular nighttime sleep. If you're on the night shift, for instance, ask your employer to switch you to the day shift. Valuing sleep may mean cutting back on all-nighters at work or school, not going out late at night, or having a babysitter available at certain hours so you can get solid sleep.

17. **Include your partner.** Ask your partner what he or she notices about your sleep patterns. Discuss anything he or she finds frightening or disruptive about your sleep. Brainstorm

ways to improve your sleep so you and your partner can sleep together. Some couples choose to get a bigger bed as a way to deal with sleep difficulties. Others make the decision not to sleep together in the same bed. Sleeping apart doesn't have to cause problems in your relationship, as long as you discuss it fully with your partner and allow time for closeness before going to sleep.

18. **Talk to a doctor.** Tell your physician about your sleep problems. You may want to track your sleep rituals and patterns—what you do or eat before you go to sleep, when you go to bed, when you wake up throughout the night, when you wake up in the morning—for a week before seeing your doctor so you can give more details about your sleep habits. Be honest with your doctor about how you've tried to improve your sleep and what you do that disrupts it. Also, share with your doctor any information that your partner knows about your sleep patterns and sleep problems. The more you tell your doctor, the more he or she can help you. Your doctor may recommend that you see a trained sleep specialist, or may prescribe medication, which can sometimes provide short-term relief for problems like insomnia.

19. **Talk to a therapist.** Another effective way to combat sleep problems is to talk to a therapist, who can help you develop better sleep habits, change unhelpful beliefs that impede your sleep, and reduce your overall stress level. Certain kinds of therapy, such as Imagery Rehearsal Therapy, can help address nightmares. In Image Rehearsal Therapy, you practice changing the endings of your nightmares while you're awake so the dreams no longer upset you. Research has shown that this type of therapy may reduce combat survivors' nightmares.

GET EXERCISE

Even though you're now safe at home, your body and mind may still be on high alert from the constant watchfulness you maintained to protect yourself and your buddies while deployed. Besides getting proper sleep, physical exercise is one of the most powerful strategies to combat this hyperalertness and to strengthen you both physically and mentally. Research indicates that a good exercise regimen produces endorphins (natural opiates) in your body. Producing endorphins can improve physical health, help combat depression, enhance mood, and reduce anxiety and stress.

Here are some helpful tips to keep in mind when you begin a regular exercise routine:

- Start your exercise regimen in consultation with a primary care physician or another professional, such as a trainer or coach.
- Don't be surprised if it takes a few trials before you get into the groove of exercising.
- Don't get discouraged. If you start a disciplined exercise program but stop it after a few weeks, don't give up. Begin again, maybe with a different kind of exercise program. Because military-style exercise such as calisthenics may remind you of the war, try other kinds of exercise such as bicycling, swimming, yoga, tennis, or aerobics.
- Identify someone to exercise with you, at least now and then. You may want to invite your partner, a family member, or a friend to join you.
- Set realistic, limited goals, especially at the beginning. If you've returned from your deployment with an injury, look for alternative exercise activities that will let you heal more rapidly. For instance, you might decide to swim rather than run if you have a leg or foot injury.
- Focus on what you enjoy about the exercise you're doing, not on what you dislike, such as the pain or discomfort. For instance, pay attention to the scenery around you if you're outdoors, the music if you use headphones, or the conversation with others if you're working out with a group.

- Reward yourself with something special after you achieve an exercise goal. Go to a movie, buy new sports equipment, or read a sports magazine.
- Remember how positive you felt about yourself both physically and mentally when you were in good shape while active in the service. Use this recollection to motivate yourself now.

Once you get used to your new exercise routine, you might find that you don't want to give it up!

EAT HEALTHILY

During your deployment, most if not all of your meals were provided without your having to shop, cook, or plan what you would eat. Now that you're home, you may find yourself eating at irregular times or turning to quick, unhealthy alternatives such as fast food or sugary snacks. Of course, maintaining a nutritious, balanced diet is an important ingredient in promoting overall health. But did you know that by carefully choosing what, when, and how much you eat you can actually help reduce unwanted feelings such as stress, anxiety, irritability, and depression? Healthy eating is another way, along with proper sleep and regular exercise, to take stronger care of yourself as you return from war and readjust to life at home.

Here are a few healthy, stress-relieving eating tips:

TIP #1

Eat a variety of foods every day, including dairy, grains, fruits, vegetables, and meat/seafood (be sure to select appropriate meat and dairy substitutes if you're a vegetarian or vegan). To get all the nutrients your body needs to combat stress and maintain health, you need to eat a balance of foods from each food group. Here's a brief list of different food types and their nutritional and emotional benefits:

- *Fiber*—whole grains, raw fruits, and vegetables can help speed your digestion and get your system back on track when stress slows your digestive system, making you feel uncomfortable and bloated.
- *Carbohydrates*—whole wheat pasta, brown rice, whole grain bread, fruits, and vegetables—can help lift depression and decrease overall stress by boosting your level of serotonin, a neurochemical responsible for your overall sense of well-being. It's important, though, to choose your carbohydrates wisely. Select those with the highest levels of nutrients and fiber.
- *Brightly colored fruits and vegetables*—orange, yellow, red, blue—help boost your immune system, which can be depressed by ongoing stress.

TIP #2

Eat three regularly scheduled meals per day, trying not to exceed 1,000 calories in any single meal. If you find that you need an extra boost in between meals, have a light snack, such as a few crackers with peanut butter or a piece of fruit and a slice of cheese. Skipping meals can cause increased irritability as your sugar levels drop. Maintaining a steady "fuel" level, on the other hand, can help to improve your energy, motivation, concentration, and mood. Eating regular meals will also help you reset your "body clock" so you can get a better night's sleep.

TIP #3

Take a multivitamin daily to ensure that you're receiving sufficient nutrients. But don't rely on vitamins to replace nutrient-rich foods. Also, avoid taking megadose vitamins (over 300 percent of the RDA), which can overload your system and cause added stress. Try to take your vitamins with your morning meal.

TIP #4

Decrease or avoid "stressful" or "depressing" foods and substances:

- *Alcohol*—Although you may have increased your drinking while overseas or since your return because you think it makes you feel "better," alcohol is actually a depressant. Excessive use can increase feelings of depression and interfere with sleep and your ability to readjust to life at home and at work. Even though certain types of alcohol, such as red wine, have been found to have health benefits, the American Medical Association recommends drinking no more than two glasses per day.

- *Caffeine and nicotine*—During your deployment you may have taken up or resumed a habit of smoking, chewing tobacco, or drinking excessive amounts of coffee or soda. While at war, these substances may have helped you keep awake, alleviate boredom, or join in with your buddies. But now that you're home and trying to come down from the experience of living in a war zone, using caffeine or nicotine only keeps you amped up, increasing your stress level and interfering with your ability to sleep.

- *Salt*—Too much salt can increase your blood pressure at a time when you need to lower your physical arousal. Avoid salty snack foods, and always taste your food before adding salt.

- *Sugar*—It's true that many healthy foods such as fruits, grains, and vegetables contain natural sugars. But eating sugar-filled snacks that aren't also rich in nutrients only revs up your system for a brief time, then soon sends it crashing down. This "sugar crash" can leave you feeling fatigued, depressed, and irritable, and it can make your body crave extra calories or sleep that it doesn't need.

- *Fats*—Although some fat—about one-third of your overall caloric intake—is essential to maintain energy and digest food properly, too much saturated fat (the kind that comes from fried foods) can stress your heart and leave you feeling tired and depressed.

ENJOY EACH EATING EXPERIENCE!

With all these "do's" and "don'ts" you may wonder whether healthy eating is more trouble than it's worth. The best way to develop and maintain good eating habits is to make sure you enjoy both the foods you eat and the way that you eat them.

When you eat out at restaurants, try to eat healthily. Some restaurant foods are filled with high fat and sugar. But there's usually something on the menu that's healthy to eat. Nowadays even fast-food chains offer healthy options like salads or meats that aren't fried or breaded.

Once in a while, allow yourself to indulge in delicious foods you like even if they're not good for you. Enjoy them in moderation, as rewards for sticking to a habit of eating well.

TALKING WITH YOUR PRIMARY CARE PHYSICIAN

Most likely, the first civilian health professional you encounter after your time in Iraq or Afghanistan will be your primary care physician (PCP), who will be interested in both your emotional and physical well-being. But many veterans returning from war are uncomfortable talking about how the experience is affecting their emotional and physical health. Some veterans think they'll be seen as complaining or "weak," so they ask few questions and reveal little about their health when talking with their PCP. Others may worry that even mentioning their problems will affect their military service. Although there's no guarantee that these things won't happen, you have to weigh the pros and cons of discussing symptoms with your PCP. If you're discharged from the service and are seeing a VA physician, everything you discuss with your doctor is confidential within the VA system of health care.

Problems don't usually disappear without intervention. Still, many health problems are not immediately obvious, even to your doctor, so you need to discuss your symptoms or concerns with him or her so you can get the right help. Your PCP can offer you treatment options for physical problems, including referring you to a specialist or prescribing medication. He or she may also be your point of entry for getting help with psychological distress and can prescribe psychiatric medication.

If you choose to talk with your PCP about your war experiences, the VA National Center for PTSD puts out a guide that can help you think about what to say. Go to www.ncptsd.va.gov/facts/specific/fs_doctor.html. If possible, download that guide before you meet with your PCP.

TIPS FOR MEETING WITH YOUR PRIMARY CARE PHYSICIAN

Besides the website information, here are some guidelines to help you prepare for your appointment with your PCP. You might not be allotted much time, so make the most of your visit.

- *Go to your PCP prepared.* Make a list of the physical and emotional concerns you have before you go to your appointment. Write down how long each problem or symptom has been bothering you, how it has affected you, and how severe it is. Prioritize your questions so that you ask the most important ones first.
- *Decide how much (if at all) you want to discuss your wartime experiences with your PCP.* You don't need to go into a lot of detail about your experiences. You can just talk about how you think your exposure to war is affecting you now in terms of your day-to-day physical and emotional health.

- *Involve your partner, a family member, or a friend in the process.* Talk with them before your appointment and, depending on the issue or issues, you may want to take them along to jot down notes and provide support. They may think of things you haven't thought to ask or mention, or they may have concerns about you that they feel are important to talk about. If you're uncomfortable taking them, you may want to ask the doctor whether you can audiotape the session so you can remember what was said and share it with loved ones later.

- *Bring any medical documents you have.* These include past medical records from the military, X-ray and MRI results, other health history records, and anything else you think will help your doctor help you.

- *List all the medications you're taking.* Write down how long you've been taking them, how often, and what dosage you take. Include over-the-counter medications, vitamins, and herbal supplements as well.

- *Be open about habits that may be harming your health.* Be honest about your alcohol and illicit drug use, as well as your caffeine and smoking habits. The doctor is trained not to judge you.

FOLLOW-UP QUESTIONS AND "FIT"

You'll probably think of more questions after you leave your PCP. Try to set up a phone appointment with him or her when you can ask those follow-up questions. Find out if there is someone else who could answer your questions if your PCP is unavailable to return your call promptly.

Sometimes the "fit" between you and your PCP is less than ideal. If you don't think the two of you can talk together honestly, ask your health care provider for a different PCP.

TIPS FOR PARTNERS, FAMILY MEMBERS, AND FRIENDS

- Carefully read through the coping strategies offered in this chapter and encourage your veteran to use them.

- Create a home environment that's good for practicing the coping skills described in this chapter. These efforts will signal to your veteran the importance of learning these strategies. For example, create a quiet area of your home where your veteran can practice the relaxation drills, or purchase him or her a pair of noise-reducing headphones.

- Sometimes, even though you have created a pleasant home environment, if your veteran lacks the motivation to get started on these new skills you may need to lead by example. And, in doing so, you can reap the benefits of reducing your own anxiety and pressures.

- Remind your veteran of his or her survival skills and strengths. Don't let him or her focus solely on what's wrong.

- Remember to use humor. Sometimes in difficult situations we forget to laugh. Laughter can be incredibly healing and can provide a sense of closeness and a broader perspective on life's challenges.

- Limit the amount of war news that you and your veteran take in at home or in the community. These efforts should include limiting war information from the television, radio, newspapers, the Internet, and other sources.

- Encourage your veteran to get good sleep by helping him or her to make a comfortable sleeping environment and establish a regular sleep schedule.

- Work with your veteran to develop a healthy plan for eating well. Cooking meals together can be a fun way to spend time, and enjoying a delicious, healthy meal can be an additional reward. If the entire family is in the habit of eating well, your veteran will be more apt to establish good eating habits too. Remember that if one member of the family isn't eating healthily, it can influence the whole family.

- Turn to other families in your community who are reuniting with veterans for support. Learn what coping strategies they are using to help with the transition. E-mail listservs and military family resources may help you find this support.

3

Coping Strategies

Now you may have a better understanding of how problems such as anxiety, depression, and alcohol abuse develop. You know more about how to spot the signs and symptoms of posttraumatic stress or phobias. But if you are (or someone you care about is) currently faced with one of these problems, what you probably want most is to know *how to fix it!* Although you can't make these war reactions disappear overnight, this chapter reveals proven strategies you can use to combat and eventually take control of your reactions.

Combating Posttraumatic Stress

In Chapter 1, you saw that it's natural for people who have experienced trauma during war to avoid anything that might remind them of the event, because these memories make them feel uncomfortable or distressed. But this kind of avoidance reinforces the symptoms of posttraumatic stress because it prevents you from learning a vital lesson: These reminders are not dangerous. They are merely "triggers" to uncomfortable memories of a past traumatic incident.

Now that you understand *why* you avoid certain activities, places, people, or situations and *how* this avoidance actually reinforces your posttraumatic stress, what can you do to stop avoiding these reminders? This chapter presents a systematic, gradual way for your body and mind to learn that the trauma is, in fact, over.

STRATEGY FOR COMBATING SITUATION AVOIDANCE

PREPARING FOR COMBAT

1. Make a list of all the triggers—activities, places, people, and situations you have been avoiding postdeployment because they remind you in some way of your experience in Iraq or Afghanistan.

2. Make another list of ways that you can reward yourself (such as dinner out, a fishing trip, a concert) after successfully using this strategy. If you'd like, ask your partner, family member, or close friend to help you with both lists.

3. Go one-by-one through each trigger on your list. Try to imagine yourself in that particular activity or situation. Then, on a Stress Scale of 0 to 10 (0 = the most relaxed you have ever felt; 10 = the most anxious or distressed you have ever felt), rate how anxious thinking about it makes you feel.

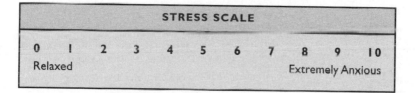

STRESS SCALE										
0	1	2	3	4	5	6	7	8	9	10
Relaxed								Extremely Anxious		

4. Rank the triggers in order. Put those with the highest Stress Scale scores at the top and those with the lowest scores at the bottom.

5. Select a trigger near the bottom of the list with a Stress Scale score of 2 or 3.

6. Make a plan to face that situation. Pick a day when you don't have other commitments such as work or social events. You

Text continued on page 74.

MATT FACES THE CHALLENGE

Remember Matt, the OIF veteran who avoided major thoroughfares and highways because they reminded him of when he was shot at while driving on busy streets in Baghdad? Over time, he realized that this avoidance was getting in the way of his ability to do the things that he wanted—and needed—to do. Here is an example of how Matt used the strategy to combat situation avoidance described on pages 71 and 74 to help his mind and body "learn" that he was no longer living in a war zone.

First Matt made a list of the traumatic war reminders that he had been avoiding since his return from Iraq:

Trigger List
❑ Busy highways and intersections
❑ Areas with a lot of pedestrian traffic
❑ Riding in the back seat of someone else's car
❑ Places where people might sit behind me (like movie theaters, restaurants)

Then Matt made a list of things or activities that he could use to reward himself after facing a trigger:

Reward List
❑ Buying a new woodworking tool
❑ Grilling a choice cut of steak
❑ Purchasing the football package on his satellite TV
❑ Upgrading his mountain bike
❑ Going out for dessert

Matt rated each situation on his trigger list from 0 to 10 on the Stress Scale and placed them in order from the most stressful to the least stressful:

Trigger Stress Ratings
❑ Areas with a lot of pedestrian traffic (Stress Scale Rating = 8)
❑ Busy highways and intersections (Stress Scale Rating = 6)

❑ Riding in the back seat of someone else's car
(Stress Scale Rating = 5)
❑ Places where people might sit behind me
(Stress Scale Rating = 3)

Matt selected the least stressful item, "places where people might sit behind me," as the first trigger to face because it had the lowest stress rating.

Matt decided to go see a movie at a small, familiar theater near his home where he had been a number of times before his deployment. He asked his best friend, Chuck, to go with him.

On his way to the theater, Matt gave himself a stress scale rating of 2. Matt chose to sit in the next-to-last row of the theater and was relieved when, as the movie was about to begin, no one had sat in the seat behind him. After the lights went out, though, a woman came in and sat behind Matt. He immediately started to feel his heart pound and his hands shake and sweat. At that point, he rated his stress at a 4. Matt used the slow-breathing technique and forced himself to sit through his uncomfortable feelings, and after about 10 minutes he felt calmer. After 30 minutes, his stress level was back down to a 2, and he actually began to enjoy the movie. Afterward, Matt and Chuck went next door and celebrated with a decadent dessert.

Over the next couple of weeks, Matt went to the same movie theater several times. He went on his own, and each time he made sure to sit closer toward the front, so that by the third visit he was near the front row with a whole audience behind him. By his fourth visit, Matt found that his stress rating at its worst, when all the other moviegoers were taking their seats behind him, was only a 2—half as much as it was the first time he had faced this trigger.

Matt decided it was time to move on to the next situation on his trigger list, "riding in the back seat of someone else's car." He knew that for this next trigger, if he went slowly, stayed in the situation even when he was uncomfortable, and repeatedly faced the trigger until his stress level had lowered, he would successfully combat and overcome another situation he had been avoiding.

may want to ask your partner, a family member, or a close friend to accompany you the first time.

7. Practice the deep breathing exercise in Chapter 2 so you're ready to use it when you face the trigger situation.

IN THE COMBAT ZONE

8. Check your Stress Scale score as you approach the situation.

9. Stay in the situation for a minimum of 30 minutes and check your Stress Scale score every 5 to 10 minutes.

10. Use the deep breathing technique to lower your physical arousal.

11. *Do not* try to distract yourself. Be as aware as possible of your surroundings and what you're thinking and feeling.

BACK ON BASE

12. Write down the Stress Scale score that you had at the time you were approaching the situation, your score at its highest point, and your score at the time that you left the situation.

13. Write down any thoughts, feelings, or physical reactions that you had while you were in the situation. Pay particular attention to what you did that helped you succeed.

14. Congratulations! You successfully faced a difficult challenge. Give yourself a reward from the list you created at the beginning of this exercise. If you've done this exercise with a partner, family member, or friend, come up with a way to include him or her in your celebration.

WINNING THE BATTLE

15. Repeat. Face the same trigger again and again at different times until your Stress Scale score at its highest point is reduced by at least 50 percent (say, until your peak score of 4 is reduced to 2).

16. When you've successfully reduced your Stress Scale score by 50 percent, move on to the next-highest trigger on your list.

COPING WITH UNWANTED IMAGES AND MEMORIES

Besides learning how to combat your avoidance of triggers, you may repeatedly have uncomfortable, upsetting memories of your time in Iraq or Afghanistan. These memories are usually about a particular event or series of events in the military that still bothers you. Sometimes they'll just pop into your mind out of the blue when you least expect them. At other times, you can predict when they might happen.

It's common for war veterans to cope by doing everything they can to avoid thinking about these disturbing images or memories. You may recall Andria from Chapter 1, who kept very busy during the day and drank heavily at night to avoid thinking about the suicide bomber who had detonated in front of her while she was stationed in Iraq.

Unfortunately, avoiding uncomfortable images or memories tends to strengthen them. The next time they come up, they surface with even more force and are harder to deal with. By avoiding them, you reinforce the belief that your memories themselves are dangerous and that the distressing incidents you experienced at war continue to be a threat. The following exercise can provide relief. It's important to master the smooth breathing exercise in Chapter 2 *before* doing this exercise.

The purpose of this exercise is to change the way you cope with unwanted images and teach you that your war memories are not dangerous. It will help you learn to create distance between yourself and the images in your mind so you can simply look at them instead of being bombarded and emotionally triggered by them. After practicing this exercise regularly, you may still "see" the images, but they'll probably be less frequent and less troubling to you.

To complete this exercise, you'll need to refer to the Stress Scale on page 71. You'll recall that it's a 0-to-10 scale where 0 is the most relaxed you've ever felt and 10 is the most anxious or distressed you've ever felt.

Do this exercise in a quiet, safe place that's free from noises and other distractions.

You'll start by practicing with an image that doesn't distress you—one you rate 0 on the scale above. For instance, you might think of eating a chocolate sundae. In your mind, watch yourself eating a chocolate sundae. By practicing this strategy with this kind of nondistressing image, you get used to the idea of thinking about yourself as separate from the image. Practice telling yourself that the image of yourself eating a chocolate sundae can come and go. Watch the image slowly disappear from your mind. Throughout the exercise, breathe slowly and remind yourself that images in your mind can't harm you. They come and they go. Different images will naturally be tied to different emotions. Some images, such as eating a chocolate sundae, can make you feel relaxed. Other images, such as those related to your military service, can lead to anxiety or even fear. But these unpleasant feelings tend to go away over time if you give them a chance. Emotions, and the images that elicit them, ebb and flow like waves. Like a wave, you can ride the anxiety that comes with an image until it subsides.

Next, practice the same exercise with a different nonmilitary image—one that brings you slight discomfort, which you've rated as a 3 on the Stress Scale. You might think of driving in traffic on a rainy day, for example. Practice inviting this image into your mind and observing it. Meanwhile, keep breathing slowly and notice how your body feels. Pay attention to the location of any muscle tension in your body. Then try to relax those particular muscles. Keep reminding yourself that the image can't harm you—it will pass on its own.

After practicing successfully with mildly distressing images, use this new skill to help you manage more upsetting images from your war service whenever they pop into your mind. Try to address only one image at a time. If your mind moves from one disturbing image to another, make yourself go back to the original image. Remind yourself that you'll get to the other images as you're ready for them. If this exercise is hard at first, don't beat yourself up. It will get easier the more you practice.

STRATEGY FOR COMBATING UNWANTED IMAGES

1. Find a quiet, safe place to do the exercise.
2. Breathe slowly and deeply.
3. Remind yourself that you're safe, and reassure yourself that the image you're going to focus on will come and go, along with the feelings related to it.
4. Now think of a slightly distressing image that you've rated as a 0 to 3 on the Stress Scale.
5. Visualizing that image, remind yourself that it can't harm you. Keep reminding yourself that all images in your mind come and go like waves—and that they're *only* images. They're not dangerous.
6. Picture the image as if you are on the platform of a train station, watching a train go past you as it moves through the station. The "train" is the image you're visualizing.
7. Next picture a more distressing image—one you've rated a 4 to 6 on the Stress Scale.
8. Practice this exercise regularly. The more you practice it, the better you'll become at handling unwanted images whenever they arise.

Combating Panic

In Chapter 1, you'll recall the example of Glen, who gave up exercise after returning home from Afghanistan because an increase in his heart rate and breathing made him feel anxious and, at times, sent him into panic attacks. His racing heart and rapid breathing from exercise were similar to the sensations that he felt when he was under threat of attack in Afghanistan so he became anxious. After experiencing a couple of panic attacks, Glen avoided exercise altogether in the hopes of preventing another attack. However, just like with Matt, Glen's avoidance was affecting his ability to do many of the things that he used to enjoy, plus he began to miss the health benefits of regular exercise.

Although Glen came to realize that he avoided exercise because his accelerated heart rate and breathing made him feel like he was in danger, as if he was back in Afghanistan, for some veterans it is not always clear which specific physical sensations are being avoided and why. Since returning from war, you may, for instance, feel anxious riding in elevators or being on a moving walkway. You may even find that merely turning your head quickly can make you suddenly feel fearful and uneasy. A certain physical sensation may be reminding you of sensations that you felt during combat and you may now be avoiding activities that bring on those anxiety-inducing sensations. As you might have already guessed, the key to ending panic is to combat the avoidance of these physical sensations. However, to do that you must first identify the specific sensations that you are avoiding. Here's how:

IDENTIFYING AVOIDED SENSATIONS

You might think of this like an allergy test: Give yourself a very small dose of a sensation to test whether or not you react to it. Following is a list of several physical sensations that commonly cause people to feel anxious or panicky, and suggested exercises for producing each reaction (borrowed from the work of Barlow & Craske, 1994). Test your reaction to each "sensation" listed below by performing one of the suggested exercises that produces it. For instance, to produce dizziness, spin in a chair for 1 minute, then rate how anxious the exercise made you feel by using the Stress Scale on page 71.

SENSATION	EXERCISE
Rapid Breathing and Heart Pounding	• Take one step up (using stairs, a box, or a footstool) and immediately step down. Do this for 1 minute at a rate fast enough to really increase your heart rate.
Dizziness	• Shake your head loosely from side to side for 30 seconds or • Spin in a chair for 1 minute.
Lightheadedness	• Place your head between your legs for 30 seconds and then lift it quickly.
Smothered Feelings/ Difficulty Breathing	• Hold your breath for as long as you can or for about 30-45 seconds, or • Holding your nostrils together to prevent air from entering through your nose, breathe through a thin straw for 1 minute, or • Sit in a hot car for 5 minutes.
Muscle Weakness/ Trembling	• Tense every part of your body, without causing pain, for 1 minute or • Hold a push-up position for as long as you can.

STRATEGY FOR COMBATING SENSATION AVOIDANCE

After you have produced each sensation listed above by doing the recommended exercises and rated each sensation on the Stress Scale on page 71, select those sensations that you assigned a stress rating of 3 or higher. Then list them in order, highest to lowest, so that the sensation that produced the highest stress rating is at the top. For instance, if you rated lightheadedness at a 10, place it at the top of your list. Now you're ready to combat your avoidance of sensations:

- Begin with the sensation at the bottom of your list, for example, the one with a stress rating of 3.
- Select one of the exercises to produce that sensation and do that exercise for a minimum of 30 seconds after you start feeling the sensation.

GLEN FACES THE CHALLENGE

Most people with panic reactions find that a number of physical sensations cause them to feel anxious. After testing his reactions to each of the sensations listed on page 79, Glen identified four sensations that he rated as a 3 or higher on the Stress Scale. Here is Glen's sensation list:

Sensation List
❑ Rapid Breathing and Heart Racing (Stress Scale Rating = 7)
❑ Difficulty Breathing (Stress Scale Rating = 6)
❑ Dizziness (Stress Scale Rating = 4)
❑ Lightheadedness (Stress Scale Rating = 3)

Although he knew in part why he avoided exercise, Glen wasn't aware of the number of uncomfortable sensations that it caused or why he also felt anxious in other seemingly unrelated situations, such as turning quickly in his desk chair. Glen began combating his avoidance of these physical sensations by first practicing the exercise that produced lightheadedness (placing his head between his legs for 30 seconds and then lifting it quickly). On the first day, he did this exercise three times, but his stress rating remained at a 3. However, on the second day, Glen's Stress Scale ratings began to decrease slightly, and by the third day, the sensation of lightheadedness, although uncomfortable, no longer made him anxious. He then moved up his list to challenge the next item, dizziness, by spinning in a chair for 1 minute at a time. He did this several times a day. Gradually, his anxiety decreased so that his stress rating was down to a 2. Glen continued tackling his sensation list until the stress rating associated with his highest ranking item was reduced by at least 50 percent. Since combating his avoidance of sensations, Glen is now back to his regular exercise routine and feeling much better both emotionally and physically.

- Repeat the exercise up to 5 times each day until your Stress Scale rating is reduced to a 2 or, at minimum, 50 percent of your original rating (for example, from a 6 to a 3), then move on to the next highest sensation item on your list.
- This is difficult work! Remember to reward yourself regularly for facing the challenge.

Combating Anger

Everyone gets angry. How you deal with your anger can make a big difference in your life. Anger can have costly consequences. Anger can damage or end relationships at home and work, lead you or others to get hurt, cause financial and legal difficulties, and wreak havoc on your health by increasing your chances of developing high blood pressure, heart disease, or stroke, as well as causing headaches or stomachaches. Here is a four-step process to help you handle your anger.

MAKE A COMMITMENT TO CHANGE

Anger can give you a sense of strength and power—feelings that are addictive. The first step to managing your anger is to identify the positive things you gain from it.

Make a list of what you *like* about your anger and what you gain from it. Here are some examples of what veterans from Iraq and Afghanistan say they like about their anger reactions:

- Anger makes me feel powerful and in charge.
- Anger protects me from feeling scared or vulnerable.
- Anger is "intoxicating"; it gives me a rush of adrenaline.
- Anger is intimidating to others.
- Anger pushes away those people I dislike or feel uncomfortable with.

Next, make a list of what you *dislike* about your anger or what you lose from it. Examples of what veterans from Iraq and Afghanistan say they dislike about their anger reactions include:

- Anger pushes away the people I care about and sometimes scares them.
- Anger makes me feel bad and guilty afterward.
- Anger may get me arrested or fired.
- Anger makes me feel out of control.
- Too much anger is bad for my physical health and body.

Now, ask yourself: If you could keep your anger reactions from ruling your life,

- How would your life be better?
- How would your opinion of yourself change?
- How would your partner's, family members', or friends' opinions of you change?
- How would your physical health be better?

Finally, compare the two lists you made earlier—the list of what you like about your anger and the list of what you dislike about it. Then ask yourself: *Do I want to change the way I react to my anger?* If your answer to this question is "yes," go ahead and move on to the next step. But if your answer is "no," you're not yet ready for the recommendations offered here. You need to be *motivated* to work on changing the way you respond to your anger. This means being ready and willing to give up the bad habit of exploding out of control when you're angry.

USE THE ANGER RULER: DON'T LET YOUR ANGER RULE YOU

This ruler provides a way to measure your reactions to your anger. A 0 on the ruler means you're feeling very calm, while a 10 indicates you're completely out of control, physically violent, or verbally abusive. Determine what it means for you to be a 5 on your ruler. (A 5 to you may not be a 5 to someone else.) Maybe a

5 is yelling at a family member when you didn't need to or giving the finger to another driver on the road. Rating your anger level on the ruler will help you understand how you behave when you're angry. The ratings will help you keep track of how close you come to letting anger rule you. The anger ruler also lets you see what situations trigger your anger so you can learn what your "red flags" are. You can also use it to measure when your anger level is lower or less intense. Then you can use some of the following strategies to control it. The better you get at knowing where your anger falls on the ruler, the quicker you'll be able to do something about your reactions.

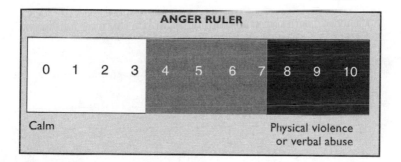

BECOME AN ANGER DETECTIVE

Every time you notice yourself becoming angry, pay close attention to your reactions, as a detective would. First, examine each situation carefully by writing down what happened. Then answer these five questions:

1. What did you do? (*behaviors/actions*)
2. What did you say out loud? (*statements/words*)
3. What did you feel? (*emotions*)
4. What were you thinking? (*thoughts*)
5. How did your body respond physically? (*physical reactions*)

Next rate where you think your anger was on the ruler by assigning a number from 0 to 10. The purpose of rating your response is to make you an observant detective so that in the future your anger won't sneak up and surprise you.

As you think back on an incident that made you angry, you'll see how each factor—actions, words, emotions, thoughts, and physical reactions—can piggyback onto the next. Think about a common traffic scenario. You're on the highway, and the car in front of you cuts you off, forcing you to slam on your breaks and yell "Watch out!" at the other driver. You think, "That guy just tried to kill me." You feel your heart rate increase, your hands become cold and clammy, and your breathing becomes shallow. Then you say to yourself, "I'm gonna get that guy," and you begin to tailgate him, creating a more dangerous situation. Each part of this scenario has the potential to fuel the next. What you think about the situation affects how you feel, which then affects what you do and say, which then fuels how your body responds physically.

The quicker you recognize each component that makes up your anger cycle, the more options you'll have to stop your anger from escalating out of control. As you picture your anger moving up the anger ruler, you'll see that fewer and fewer options are available to you at each stage. You're less able to choose to lower your anger, and you experience "physiological flooding"—that is, your body becomes physically overwhelmed to the point that your hands or brow sweat, your blood pressure or heart rate increase, you can't think clearly, you feel out of control or paralyzed, or you have a full-blown panic attack or violent outburst.

LEARN FROM YOUR MISTAKES

At those times when you realize later that you didn't like the way you reacted to your anger, seize the opportunity to learn from your mistakes. Ask yourself the five questions below and write down your responses.

1. What could I have done to help decrease my anger? (*behaviors/actions*)

2. What could I have said to help decrease my anger? (*statements/words*)

3. What could I have felt to decrease my anger? (*emotions*)

4. What could I have thought to help decrease my anger? (*thoughts*)

5. What could I have done to help decrease the tension in my body? (*physical reactions*)

You may find that changes in any one of these areas would have changed the outcome of the situation. Just as these factors can snowball together to cause you difficulties, they can also work together to provide solutions. In the traffic scenario, when the driver cut you off, if you had said to yourself, "Wow, that guy must be having a bad day," it might have triggered a whole different set of feelings and behaviors. Instead of taking the driver's actions personally, you could recognize that his behaviors are *about him—not you*. Go ahead and brainstorm alternative ways of behaving, talking, feeling, thinking, and physically reacting soon after a situation upsets you. Although it may be harder to do at such times, you'll be more likely to use these strategies the next time a difficult situation arises.

KNOW YOUR "RED FLAG MOMENTS"

Particular issues or situations that upset you more easily than others are called "red flag moments." Making a list of these red flag moments can prepare you to be on the alert for an intense reaction of anger before it happens. You can then prevent it altogether by planning what anger strategies you'll use in each of these situations. Here are some red flag moments that veterans from Iraq and Afghanistan have said trigger their anger. Use these examples to make your own list:

- Driving
- Children crying
- Large crowds
- Sudden loud noises like horns honking
- Long lines

- Your partner, family members, or friends not listening to you
- Feeling disrespected
- Frustrations at work (for example, having to follow instructions from your boss)
- Taking the bus
- Experiencing racism or sexism
- Waiting for medical appointments

FIND THE STRATEGIES THAT WORK FOR YOU, AND PRACTICE THEM

Which strategies can you pull out of your coping toolbox to help keep anger from ruling you? Here's a list of strategies that veterans from Iraq and Afghanistan have used to help them rule their anger instead of being ruled by it. Choose strategies from this list or other techniques you already know that work for *you*. Then make and keep your own list of strategies to combat your anger reactions. Regularly practicing the strategies on this list will pay off in the long run: You'll learn to take control of your anger.

COMBAT STRATEGIES FOR RULING ANGER

- Pay attention to your breathing, slow it down, and take deep breaths.
- Notice any tension in your body and try to relax that part of your body by stretching or massaging it.
- Take a "time-out" from the situation when you're feeling flooded. Often the best technique for calming down, a time-out is when you physically leave a situation before you say or do anything destructive. Depending on the situation, you may want to tell the other person that you're taking a time-out: "I need to leave right now. I'll be back in

____ minutes." If you use a time-out, don't plan on getting back into the upsetting situation for at least 30 minutes. During the time away, use strategies to calm down; don't try to justify why you were angry.

- Be assertive, *not* aggressive, about what you want. Express yourself directly and firmly while respecting the other person. Being assertive earns you respect because you ask for what you want in a way that doesn't make the other person feel small or humiliated. Being aggressive earns you enemies because you try to get what you want by intimidating, threatening, or being violent.
- When speaking about a situation, speak for yourself; don't tell others what they're thinking or feeling.
- Say reassuring statements to yourself to help calm down.
- Remind yourself that the issues at hand are not life-threatening.
- Talk to a friend about what's upsetting you.
- Buy yourself time when responding. Delay your response until you've taken control of your anger.
- Write down the thoughts and feelings you have about the situation.
- Practice how you'll deal with a difficult situation in advance by rehearsing with a partner, family member, or friend.
- Don't just look at the times when things didn't go well. Instead, recall the times when you handled a difficult situation well and use them to remind yourself that you can handle your anger. Your success with these situations may provide you with clues that can aid you in handling other difficult situations in the future.

Remember, the more you practice these strategies, the better you'll be able to handle your anger reactions.

Text continued on page 90.

BILL FACES THE CHALLENGE

In Chapter 1, you read about Bill and his problems with anger. Even though his anger had gotten so out of control that it landed him in jail, he—like many returning veterans—liked the way that it made him feel, alive and powerful. But Bill was concerned enough about keeping his job and his family that he decided to not let his anger reactions rule his life. So he started by making a list of what he liked and disliked about his reactions to his anger:

LIKES AND DISLIKES ABOUT MY ANGER

Likes
- It gives me a rush, makes me feel "pumped."
- It makes me feel strong, like I can face anything.
- It makes people pay attention to me.

Dislikes
- It frightens my wife and kids.
- It gets me in trouble (I could lose my job or go to jail).
- Sometimes I feel out of control.

Bill then asked himself the following questions and wrote down his answers:
- *How would my life be better?* I would get along better with my boss and my wife. My kids might want to be around me more. I wouldn't have to worry about getting into legal trouble.
- *How would my opinion of myself change?* I would feel more in control, and I'd feel that I was treating the people I care about better. I would just feel like a better person.
- *Would my family's opinion of me change?* My wife says she would feel closer to me instead of pushed away. She and the kids wouldn't feel like they had to "tip-toe" around me all the time so they might want to spend more time with me.
- *Would other aspects of my life be better?* I'd probably feel better—not so stressed and on edge. Maybe my blood pressure would even come down.

After answering these questions and comparing his list of likes and dislikes, Bill decided that he was ready to begin combating his anger. He began by carefully observing his own reactions following a situation in which he became intensely angry. He became an "anger detective."

ANGER OBSERVATIONS: BEING AN EMOTION DETECTIVE

Situation: A coworker accidentally spilled some of his coffee onto my shoe. I yelled, called him an idiot, and then left the meeting.
Anger Ruler Rating = 6

WHAT HAPPENED

What I did (behaviors): I yelled and stormed out of the room.
What I said (statements/words): "You idiot!"
What I felt (emotions): Unsure, maybe scared, very irritated and annoyed.
What I thought (thoughts): That idiot is so clumsy. He could make a serious mistake.
What I felt in my body (physical reactions): I tightened my arms and fists like I was going to hit him, and I could feel my heart racing.

WHAT COULD I HAVE DONE DIFFERENTLY?

What could I have done to decrease my anger? (behaviors): I could have taken a time-out.
What could I have said to decrease my anger? (statements/words): I could have made a joke about it like: "My shoe doesn't drink coffee, it would prefer some water."
What could I have thought that would have decreased my anger? (thoughts): It was an accident—he didn't do it on purpose. Anyone could make that mistake. It doesn't mean that he's dangerous to be around.
What could I have done to help decrease the tension in my body? (physical reactions): I could have done some deep breathing or concentrated on relaxing my arms and hands.

Being an anger detective helped Bill see the ways he could have controlled his anger toward his colleague and avoided the embarrassment of storming out of the meeting. After that, Bill became more aware of his thoughts, emotions, behaviors, verbal comments, and physical reactions at the time of his angry outbursts, which made it easier for him to take control. He became aware that anyone making a mistake (including himself) was a real trigger for him. And he discovered that practicing strategies such as deep breathing and muscle relaxation at times when he was alone and calm made it more likely that he'd use them during times of anger. Gradually, Bill's relationships at work and home improved as people began to feel more comfortable around him and to enjoy his sense of humor.

Combating Alcohol or Drug Abuse

Many people drink or use drugs because of the positive feelings it provides, but it can cause tremendous problems in their lives, including family difficulties, unexplained work absences, and legal troubles. Like with anger, the first step toward controlling substance use is to acknowledge that in spite of the good feelings it produces, your drinking or drug use is causing problems in your life.

ARE YOU MOTIVATED TO CONTROL YOUR DRINKING OR DRUG USE?

This section will help you gauge how motivated you are to decrease or stop your use of alcohol or drugs. Then you'll have a chance to ask yourself questions that will help you make a plan. Stopping or controlling your substance use can be the first step toward helping yourself overcome other deployment-related problems. In fact, if you don't first take control of your drinking or drug use, it will be very hard to confront other problems such as posttraumatic stress, depression, or anger.

This section is filled with questions. You may be the type of person who'll read and answer every single question, or you may only answer a couple of them. Either way, this section will provide you with useful tips on how to accomplish your particular goals.

DO YOU HAVE A SUBSTANCE USE PROBLEM?

The first step in taking control of your alcohol or drug use is to see whether you think you have a substance use problem. You may be reluctant to consider this possibility. Some people aren't yet ready to decrease or stop their use. You may be in that category. Maybe there haven't been enough reasons for you to stop. Maybe your reasons for drinking or taking drugs are too powerful for you to stop. If you're willing to *just consider* the possibility of decreasing or stopping your use, it may be helpful to answer the following questions. If you're not currently interested in changing the way you use alcohol or drugs, you may want to stop here and consider rereading this section if you change your mind.

REASONS FOR DRINKING OR USING DRUGS

Here are some reasons that veterans from Iraq or Afghanistan have given for why they drink or use drugs:

- ❑ It helps me get to sleep.
- ❑ It helps me block out bad memories of the war.
- ❑ It helps me feel like I fit in.
- ❑ It helps me have fun.

Start by making a list of the reasons you drink or use drugs. Here are some questions that might help you:

- What do you like about your substance use?
- How has it helped you cope?
- What do you like about the effects?
- What would you miss about using if you were to stop?
- What other aspects of your using are important to you?

REASONS FOR NOT DRINKING OR USING DRUGS

Now, here are some reasons that other veterans have given about why they should decrease or stop their drug or alcohol use:

- ❑ It's ruining my relationships with family and friends.
- ❑ My hangovers have made it hard to go to work or take care of other responsibilities.
- ❑ Buying alcohol or drugs is costing me a lot of money.
- ❑ I sometimes get out of control or embarrass myself when I drink or use drugs.
- ❑ Sometimes when I'm drunk or high, I do things that are dangerous or illegal, like driving a car much faster than the speed limit.
- ❑ It's bad for my health.

Make a list of the reasons why you should decrease or stop your drug or alcohol use. Here are some questions that might help you:

- How does using substances prevent you from achieving your goals?
- What difficulties do you encounter from using alcohol or drugs?
- What are some advantages of decreasing or stopping your use?
- Do you get annoyed when others talk about your drinking or drug use?
- Is using alcohol or drugs impacting your health?
- Are you willing to engage in any medical tests (such as liver function tests) to make sure your health isn't being compromised because of your use?
- Is your alcohol or drug use impacting your family, school, or work?
- Is it getting you in trouble with the law or costing you too much money?
- Are other areas in your life being affected by your use?
- If you continue to use at your current rate, what will life be like for you in 5 years? 10 years? 20 years?

If you can, discuss your list and answers with your partner, a family member, or a close friend. Then listen to his or her ideas about your substance use.

After answering these questions and reviewing your lists, you'll probably find that you fall into one of the following four categories:

1. "I don't have a problem and don't intend to change my alcohol or drug use."
2. "I'm not sure if I want to stop my alcohol or drug use."
3. "I would like to decrease or stop my alcohol or drug use."
4. "I have already decreased or stopped my alcohol or drug use."

"I DON'T HAVE A PROBLEM."

If you fall into category 1, you're at a place where you don't want to decrease or give up your substance use. If this is the case, review the above questions periodically (about once a month) to make sure you remain comfortable with your decision. In fact, you may see your substance use as a solution rather than as a problem. Remember Joe from our earlier example? He didn't consider his substance use a problem . . . yet.

"I'M NOT SURE IF I WANT TO STOP."

If you fall into category 2, you have mixed feelings about decreasing or stopping your use. Answer the questions below to better understand what your thoughts are about decreasing or stopping.

- Why do you want to decrease or stop your alcohol or drug use?
- Why *don't* you want to decrease or stop your alcohol or drug use?
- What needs to happen to convince you that it's time to decrease or stop your alcohol or drug use?
- Do your family or friends think it's a good idea for you to decrease or stop your alcohol or drug use? What have they seen that makes them think that decreasing or stopping is a good idea?
- Have you decreased or stopped your alcohol or drug use in the past? If so, what helped you do it?
- What would help this time?
- On a scale of 0 to 10, with 0 being not at all interested in decreasing or stopping your use and 10 being intensely interested in decreasing or stopping your use, where are you now?

DESIRE TO STOP SCALE										
0	1	2	3	4	5	6	7	8	9	10
No desire to stop								Intense desire to stop		

- What would it take for you to move from where you are on this scale to the next step closer to 10?
- Are you willing to take that next step? Why or why not?

Conduct an experiment. If you're not sure about decreasing or stopping your use, you may want to experiment with trying not to use drugs or alcohol for a period of time, to compare the difference in your life between using and not using. Ask your partner, family members, or friends what you're like when you're not using substances. What do they notice that is positive? What do they notice that is negative?

Some people feel worse when they first stop using. Some veterans report feeling depressed or irritable or having more powerful memories from the war when they stop. These problems will improve over time. Trying not to use for a period of time will also give you information about how easy or hard it may be to stop. You don't have to stop forever to conduct the experiment.

"I WOULD LIKE TO DECREASE OR STOP."

If you fall into category 3, you have decided you want to decrease or stop your use of alcohol or drugs. Answer the questions below to help you continue on this path:

- Now that you've decided to stop, what is the next small step toward making this a reality in the next few days? What will you need to say or do to make it happen?
- On a scale from 0 to 10, with 0 being "not likely" and 10 being "very likely," how likely is it that you'll accomplish the next step toward decreasing or stopping your use?

LIKELIHOOD OF STOPPING SCALE
0 1 2 3 4 5 6 7 8 9 10
Not likely   Very likely

- If you're not at a 9 or 10, what do you need to say or do to move up to the next step on the scale?

- Whom can you count on in your life to support you in this process?
- How do you think your life will be different if you decrease or stop using?

"I HAVE DECREASED OR STOPPED."

If you fall into category 4, you have successfully stopped or decreased your use of alcohol or drugs, at least temporarily. Congratulations! Now answer the questions below to help you stay free from alcohol or drugs:

- How were you able to make this change?
- Who helped you, and will they continue to do so?
- What are the benefits of decreasing or not using alcohol or drugs?
- What do you miss the most about using substances?
- What are you most proud of, now that you've stopped or decreased your use?
- What red flags might trigger you to pick up and use again? What steps have you taken to deal with these triggers?
- Are you using Alcoholics Anonymous (AA), Narcotics Anonymous (NA), or another recovery program to help? Why or why not?
- What do you think you need to do to maintain this change?

DON'T GIVE UP!

For most veterans, stopping or decreasing their alcohol or drug use is an extremely challenging task. Some of you may need to try several times before you achieve success. You may find that your first attempts at stopping temporarily bring on *more* difficulties with your family. Don't let these temporary problems keep you from achieving your goal. And don't lose hope if you're not able to immediately achieve your goals. Be creative and use whatever resources will help you succeed. That could mean reading

DANNY FACES THE CHALLENGE

Remember Danny, the firefighter who binged on alcohol a couple of times a week? After asking himself the questions listed at the beginning of this section, he came up with the following list of reasons for drinking vs. reasons for controlling his drinking:

Reasons for Drinking
- It helps me feel less jumpy.
- It helps me get to sleep.
- It helps me forget about the war

Reasons for Controlling My Drinking
- I'm late or miss work because I'm hungover.
- I miss family events because I'm too drunk.
- I argue more with my wife and yell at my kids when I'm drinking.
- It "weighs me down" and keeps me from exercising.

Because alcohol helped Danny cope with problematic war reactions like feeling jumpy and having bad war memories, he felt unsure at first about giving up his drinking. But the questions and his list helped him think about how alcohol was causing him problems. He was especially concerned about what his wife thought, so he shared the questions and his list with her. Boy, did she have something to say about it!

Danny conducted an experiment by not drinking for two weeks. Although it was sometimes hard for him not to pick up a drink when he felt nervous or was having trouble sleeping, he was surprised at how his relationship with his wife and kids and his performance at work improved. When he made a commitment to stop drinking and followed through on it, his family went from having little respect for him to being extremely proud. Of course, it wasn't easy, but he found an AA group where he was comfortable and got an AA sponsor who was also a war veteran. To Danny's surprise, the guys at his firehouse were very supportive. They even started hanging out with him at restaurants instead of bars.

this chapter a few times and then setting a goal with your partner, family members, or a friend. Or you may want to find a buddy who's also interested in decreasing or stopping his or her substance use and work together on this goal. Other solutions may include attending AA or NA meetings, getting involved in outpatient treatment, enrolling in residential or inpatient treatment, or doing a combination of the above. The key is to keep trying and not give up!

Combating Depression

Inactivity and negative thoughts can lead to a cycle of depression. In this section you'll find step by step exercises and tips to increase your activity and decrease your negativity. Then you can learn once again to enjoy life and feel good about yourself.

GET ACTIVE

If you're currently feeling depressed, the prospect of getting active can seem at best unappealing and at worst overwhelming. Not only do you feel unmotivated to do anything, but you're fairly certain that if you did, you simply wouldn't enjoy it. Besides, even if you wanted to get active, you can't think of anything to do. Of course, it's your depression that's causing you to feel this way, and your inactivity is actually working to make you even more depressed. So how do you break out of these chains of inactivity? Here is an exercise that will help you do it.

CREATE AN ACTIVITY LIST

1. Write down activities that you recall having enjoyed in the past. Here are some examples:
   - Bowling
   - Watching sports "live"

- Going to a movie
- Doing crossword puzzles
- Having lunch with a friend
- Going fishing or hunting
- Going out to dinner
- Riding your bike or motorcycle

As you see, your list should include very simple things like making popcorn and renting a movie, as well as more involved activities like going on a rafting trip. If you're having difficulty creating this list, ask your partner, family member, or a friend who knows you well to help.

2. Next to each activity, on a scale of 0 to 5, rate how much you think you'd enjoy doing it based on your past experience. You may actually be doing some of these things now but not enjoying them as much as you did before you felt depressed. Be sure to rate each activity according to how much you remember enjoying it before you were depressed.

3. Make a list of activities you think you might enjoy, even though you've never done them. You might start by completing the sentence "I've always wanted to . . . " Here are some examples:

- Take a cooking class
- Go to a certain concert or show
- Take a hike on a trail you've read about
- Take a drive to a town you've wanted to visit for years

After you've made this list, rate each activity on the enjoyment scale according to how much you *imagine* you might enjoy it.

ENJOYMENT SCALE					
0	1	2	3	4	5
Not enjoyable					Very enjoyable

PLAN YOUR ACTIVITIES

Now that you have two lists of enjoyable activities—one of activities you used to enjoy and the other of activities you've never tried but think you'd enjoy—the next step is to do some of them. If you're depressed, this is not so simple. For one thing, you tend to think that just because you enjoyed a particular activity in the past doesn't mean you will now. In fact, you probably won't find as much enjoyment in doing the things you used to do. But it's also true that the less you do, the less you will enjoy anything. Since doing activities requires energy and motivation—two resources that are in short supply for anyone who's depressed—you'll need to put more thought and effort into doing even the simplest things. This means *planning*.

PREPARE AN ACTIVITY SCHEDULE

The key to getting active when you're feeling depressed is to schedule and commit yourself to doing enjoyable activities. As strange as it seems, when you're in a depressed mood, you actually need to force yourself to do things that you once enjoyed or might enjoy. Even the small things, like reading a good book or taking a hot bath or shower, need to be scheduled into your day to ensure that you actually do them. So get out your calendar (or buy or make yourself a calendar).

1. Start with the current month. Review the activities on your two lists and consider those that you rated as 2 or higher on the enjoyment scale that can be done easily or every day. On the days when you're working or have other commitments, schedule at least one of these activities to do at the beginning of your day (say, making your favorite breakfast), at the end of your day (a hot bath or shower), or during your lunch break (having lunch with a friend). If possible, try to schedule more than one small, enjoyable activity per day.

2. Consider those activities on your two lists that you rated at a 2 or higher but that are more involved in terms of time, resources, and planning. Schedule one per week. These activities may be no more complex than going on a picnic; they simply may require a greater level of energy and motivation on your part to do them. For these more complex activities, it's important to involve at least one other person, not only to help you make it happen but also to enjoy it with you.

3. Review your calendar on a daily basis and, after completing each activity, rate it on the enjoyment scale and mark your rating on the calendar. Remember, you need to actually schedule these enjoyable activities into your life. That means marking it on your calendar for a particular date at a particular time and then keeping that appointment just as you would a staff meeting or a doctor's visit.

After a week or so, if you've kept your activity appointments, you should find that your ability to do things and even to enjoy them has improved. You may even find yourself doing enjoyable activities that aren't on your schedule, and you may think of new activities to add to your lists. Continue to plan like this for each month. The funny thing is, even though you're using more energy, you will actually find yourself feeling less tired and lethargic. That's because you're starting to break the cycle of depression.

COMBAT NEGATIVE THINKING

Along with inactivity, negative thinking works to maintain the cycle of depression. When you're depressed, the negative thoughts seem to come automatically, as if they're out of your control. In a sense, your negative thinking has gotten out of your control, like a bad habit that's difficult—but not impossible—to break. As with most habits, the first step toward combating negative thinking is to become more aware of what it is and when, how, and why it happens.

UNDERSTANDING NEGATIVE THINKING

Sure, you've heard people say things like "Oh, he's just a pessimist" or "He's always so negative," but what *is* negative thinking, really? In depression, common thought patterns lead people to see others, themselves, and the world in a negative light. Here are some of the more common ways of thinking that feed the cycle of depression:

- Drawing conclusions when evidence is lacking or even contradictory ("I was useless as a medic" when, in fact, dozens of soldiers under your care were saved).

- Exaggerating or minimizing the meaning of an event. You blow things out of proportion or shrink their importance immediately. ("My boss didn't like the idea that I presented. She thinks I'm a real idiot" when she actually incorporated aspects of your idea into a larger plan.)

- Disregarding important aspects of a situation ("I didn't get that job because I don't interview well," when you actually were overqualified for the position).

- Seeing things as black-or-white. You oversimplify events, situations, or characteristics as either good or bad, right or wrong. ("Rosalinda's great at making friends—I'm terrible at it.")

- Overgeneralizing from a single incident. You view a negative event as a never-ending pattern of defeat ("I yelled at my son today—I'm a horrible father").

- Emotional reasoning: You reason things out based on how you feel. ("He knocked over my beer just to piss me off.")

Of course, being depressed doesn't mean that you routinely use every one of these negative thinking patterns, but most people who are depressed habitually use two or three. If you're going to break the habit of negative thinking, first you need to identify the patterns you commonly use and the situations in which you're most likely to use them. This level of awareness will let you start to interrupt your negative thoughts and challenge them.

IDENTIFYING AND CHALLENGING YOUR THOUGHTS

Below is a list of questions you can use to become aware of your negative thinking patterns and then challenge them. Begin by considering a thought or belief you have about yourself or a particular situation, such as "I'm a horrible father" or "I was useless as a medic." Then ask yourself each question. Keep in mind that not every question may apply to a particular thought or belief.

CHALLENGING QUESTIONS
1. What is the evidence for and against this thought or belief?

MITCH FACES THE CHALLENGE

Remember Mitch, the Navy medic who became depressed after returning from Iraq? Mitch became less and less active, eventually spending much of his time in bed and having thoughts that he was a failure. Mitch had to do something to break the cycle of depression he was stuck in. His first step was to find a therapist who, along with his family, helped him create a list of activities he had enjoyed before his deployment. Mitch then rated his level of enjoyment for each activity and began entering activities into a monthly calendar. Although it was hard at first, he pushed himself to keep the activity appointments that he had scheduled.

- On Monday, he watched a football game on TV.
- On Tuesday, he read an article in one of his sports magazines that had been piling up.
- On Wednesday, he had planned to have breakfast at his favorite diner, but found it too difficult to get out of bed. That night he pushed himself to go out for ice cream instead.
- On Thursday night, Mitch read a couple of more magazine articles.
- On Friday, he had lunch with his sister.

2. *What are the odds that my thought or belief is accurate (100 percent, 50 percent, 10 percent)?*
3. *Am I thinking in all-or-nothing, black-or-white terms?*
4. *Am I using words or phrases that are extreme or exaggerated (like always, forever, never, have to, must, can't, every time)?*
5. *Am I focusing on small details instead of the entire picture?*
6. *Are my judgments based on feelings instead of facts?*

EXAMINING YOUR THOUGHTS

The next step in breaking the habit of negative thinking is to examine the thoughts you have when certain situations arise. Then you can use the same questions to challenge and change your negative thinking. Here is a list of questions to help you

> For the weekend, Mitch had planned to meet some friends at a sports bar to watch a game. As the time got closer, though, he felt more depressed. "I'll never be able to get out of the house," he thought. "I'm such a loser that I can't even drive a couple miles to hang out with my friends." Then one of his friends called and offered to pick him up. Mitch forced himself to say "yes" even though he didn't want to. By the end of the game, he was glad he had gone and he rated his enjoyment level at a 3. When he thought back about the week, he noticed that he actually felt less tired and didn't need to spend as much of his time in bed as before.
>
> Using the challenging questions asked in this section, Mitch also began to address his negative thoughts, especially the belief that he was a failure. He realized that he had successfully helped and saved a good number of Marines in Iraq. He also saw that when someone died, it wasn't because of his incompetence, but because of the severity of their wounds and the time it took for him to get to their location. Mitch gradually learned to examine his thoughts while he was having them. Then he could challenge them with alternative thoughts that were more positive and realistic. In time, Mitch felt less depressed and had more energy and motivation to look for a job and spend time with friends.

keep track of your negative thoughts and the ways you have challenged them.

- Describe the situation. ("I was cut off in traffic.")
- What were my negative thoughts? ("People hate me because of the car I drive"; "I'm always the one to get cut off.")
- What questions did I ask myself to challenge my negative thoughts?
- Am I exaggerating? ("Yes—I don't get cut off that often.")
- What is the evidence that he cut me off because of the car I drive? ("None, plus someone else was on the road at the time with the same kind of car and *he* wasn't cut off.")
- What alternative thoughts did I have? ("The guy was probably just in a hurry and didn't even notice me.")

SHOULD YOU SEEK PROFESSIONAL HELP?

If you're having emotional problems related to your war experience that are lasting a long time, causing you a lot of stress, or interfering with your life, you should consider seeing a professional for help.

If you're feeling suicidal or homicidal, you should seek help immediately by calling 911, visiting your closest emergency room, or by calling one of the numbers provided in the "Resources" section at the back of this book.

Here is general information about who therapists are and what types of therapy may help you and your loved ones, as well as how medication can sometimes be used to help with emotional problems.

WHO ARE THERAPISTS?

Therapists are trained specialists, such as psychologists, social workers, psychiatrists, marriage and family therapists, or other mental health professionals, who have received education and training in therapy and are licensed in your state. Therapists can also be pastoral or church counselors, vocation rehabilitation counselors, career counselors, or life coaches. School counselors can be another source of support for your children.

WHAT IS THERAPY?

Therapy is a service that people use to help cope with emotional, relationship, or vocational problems. It involves talking to a trained professional like those mentioned above to identify the source of problems and help overcome or manage them. It often focuses on feelings, thoughts, behaviors, and past experiences that are currently causing problems. Therapy helps people reduce their stress and improve their lives so they're more at peace. Talking with a therapist can help you feel supported so you can make changes in your life and feel happier. Remember, going to a therapist for help doesn't mean you're crazy or weak, even though this is a common myth in the military. Getting help for yourself and loved ones actually requires strength and courage.

As a returning veteran, you can use therapy as a tool to help you readjust to home and cope with the difficult war-related reactions you may be experiencing. Therapy can help with a wide range of problems veterans experience after war, such as depression, posttraumatic stress, relationship difficulties, anger, grief, guilt, overuse of alcohol or drugs, parenting issues, and work and school concerns. Your partner, family members, and friends may also want to consider individual therapy to cope with their reactions to your return, or you may want to go together. Therapy usually involves meeting with a therapist at the same time every week or every other week. In most cases, you and your therapist will work out a therapy schedule and decide how long you'll meet for each session and how many sessions you'll attend.

What is said in therapy between you and your therapist is usually considered confidential, with a few legal exceptions. If you're still in the service, however, you'll want to know whether the military has access to your therapy records. It's important to trust your therapist so that you can be honest about your problems and talk about any strong reactions you may be having to his or her approach.

TYPES OF THERAPY

Most therapy falls into four basic categories: individual therapy, group therapy, couples therapy, and family therapy.

In individual therapy, you and a therapist talk for 50 to 60 minutes per session about specific problems you're having, ways to handle them, and goals for your time in therapy, such as discovering the sources of problems and learning to break old habits. Some therapists may give homework assignments to complete between sessions. The objective is to apply what you learn in individual therapy to your personal and work relationships.

In group therapy, you and a small number of other people— usually 5 to 10—meet with 1 or 2 therapists regularly for 60 to 90 minutes per session to talk about similar kinds of problems, how these problems are affecting you today, and ways to cope with them. Group therapy often helps members discover that they're not the only one struggling with a particular problem. Not feeling so alone can be a source of relief in itself. Group therapy can be a safe place to receive support and feedback from the therapists and other members, and this can help you learn to trust other people. Group therapy can offer benefits that individual therapy may not furnish, though you won't receive as much individual attention.

In couples therapy, you and your partner meet with 1 or 2 therapists for 60 to 90 minutes per session to work together on your relationship. Often the focus is on improving your communication; you learn new ways to talk to each other and break old patterns. You may also learn how to better balance each other's roles and needs, as well as how to show one another respect, support, and appreciation. Couples therapy can be an excellent place to discuss issues involving connecting with each other after separation and serving in a war.

In family therapy, the whole family meets with 1 or 2 therapists for 60 to 90 minutes per session to talk about difficulties in family relationships. The focus is on improving how you and family members interact with each other and changing unhealthy family patterns that fuel each other's stress and cause problems in the family system. Both couples therapy and family therapy can be very helpful because they recognize that problems exist between people, not only within the individual.

CHOOSING A THERAPIST

If you're like most men and women who have served in the military, you may have never seen a therapist (except maybe a military mental health specialist or chaplain), and the thought of finding one may seem overwhelming. You know, for instance, that if you're having trouble with your foot, you should see a podiatrist—but how do you know what type of therapist is right for you?

Current research indicates that no one educational degree or type of training (for example, psychologist, social worker, psychiatrist, marriage and family therapist) is better than any other. Whatever type of therapist you choose, though, it's absolutely essential that you make sure he or she is licensed to practice psychotherapy in your state. The next most important factor in picking a therapist is the level of experience he or she has, both overall and in working with people like you. Search for someone who has experience working with war veterans and also in the specific area of your concern. For instance, if you're grieving the loss of a buddy, find a therapist with experience in helping people with grief and loss.

Another primary ingredient for a good therapy experience is the level of comfort you feel with your therapist. Although it takes time to develop a real connection with any therapist, before making your choice you'll want to consider some basic issues, such as whether you'd feel more comfortable with a male or a female therapist; whether you'd prefer going to a hospital, an out-patient clinic, or a small private practice therapy suite; and whether the ethnicity or religion of the therapist is important to you. Some therapists allow a brief initial visit, often free, so you can see how comfortable the fit is for you both.

If you're living in a small community or you have minimal or no insurance coverage, you may not have the luxury of choice. If your insurance provider or employee assistance program does cover therapy, they can give you a list of therapists or refer you to a list on the Web, leaving you with the responsibility of deciding whom to choose. If so, remember that you're the consumer. A therapist, like any other professional, is there to provide a service, so it's up to you to determine whom you'd like to work with and whether you're feeling satisfied with the service that he or she is providing. You wouldn't, for instance, take your Ford pickup to a Jaguar specialist, nor would you continue to go back to a mechanic you weren't satisfied with. Your emotional health, of course, is vastly more important than how your car runs. If it takes visits to more than one therapist to find the right one, that's okay; you may need to shop around.

When looking for a therapist, here are a few questions you may want to ask him or her before starting:
- What are your credentials (where are you licensed)?
- What's your experience in dealing with war veterans (and their families)?
- What's your experience working with people with my problem (say, depression, anger, marital problems, alcohol abuse, or grief and loss)?

- What type of therapy approach do you usually use (for example, directive, skills-based, mostly listening, homework assignments, talking about the past)?
- Do you take insurance (are you on my insurance panel)?
- What do you charge and how do you collect payments?
- How often would we meet and how long is each session?
- How long do you expect me to be in therapy with you?
- What results do you usually see?
- If I need a mental health service that isn't offered by you or your clinic, such as medication, how will you help me obtain it?

Finally, remember that after you've chosen a therapist, if you feel uncomfortable with him or her during the course of therapy, it's important to talk about your reactions. You and your therapist may be able to talk through your concerns about working together. Instead of ending therapy abruptly and prematurely, you may find that the results are greatly improved once you make your needs and concerns clear.

WHAT ABOUT MEDICATION?

Besides therapy, medication may also help improve your emotional well-being. Doctors (including psychiatrists, primary care physicians, general practitioners, and internists), as well as nurse practitioners and some psychologists in certain states, can prescribe these medications. Like therapy, medication is one tool you have at your disposal to help you cope with readjustment problems. If you decide to take medication, you should work carefully with the health professional prescribing it to find the best relief for your individual condition.

It's extremely important to be aware of the possible side effects of your medication, monitor whether you're experiencing them, assess how well you feel on the medication, and then communicate this information to the health professional prescribing it. With some medications, blood tests and other readings are required regularly. It's essential to follow the medication guidelines given to you by the health professional who has prescribed it. If you decide to go off the medication, consult with him or her first, because withdrawal reactions can be serious. Follow-up visits with your health professional are essential when you're on a medication.

Individuals react differently to psychiatric medications. You may have to try several types of medication before you find the right one for you, and you may need to take more than one medication (often called a "cocktail") to adequately address all your problems. The goal is to find the most effective medication for reducing your symptoms that also minimizes troublesome side effects. Some medications can provide immediate relief from acute levels of distress, like when you've just returned home from the war zone or have received bad news about the loss of a buddy and can't sleep. Other medications can take four to six weeks, or even longer, to reach their full effect, so you need to be patient as you begin taking a new medication. It's well established that medication works best when combined with therapy.

TIPS FOR PARTNERS, FAMILY MEMBERS, AND FRIENDS

- Be aware of any signs of difficulties your veteran is having. Reading this chapter will help you detect problems like posttraumatic stress, depression, or substance abuse, and you may see the signs before your veteran does. If you notice any of these behaviors and symptoms in your veteran, come up with strategies for getting him or her help. The strategies you use will depend on your relationship with him or her and your veteran's ability to admit difficulties and seek help. You may want to encourage your veteran to read this chapter and then talk about how he or she is feeling. It may take a number of talks before your veteran is willing to admit he or she has a problem and needs help.

- If your veteran is talking about death or suicide or showing signs of wanting to harm himself/herself or someone else (for example, loading a weapon with ammunition and keeping it in the home), take these threats seriously and get help at your local hospital's emergency room or by calling 911.

- Don't take your veteran's "different" or "difficult" behaviors personally. In other words, don't blame yourself for his or her problems. Remember that you didn't *cause* these difficulties.

- Many veterans will have a bumpy recovery road. Be prepared for relapses along the way. Don't let the bumps in the road leave you feeling hopeless.

- Reduce stress in your own life. If your veteran is displaying any of the problems described in this chapter, the odds are that you feel stressed too, and you may not be able to accomplish all the tasks you previously did. Prioritize what tasks are important and attempt to accomplish them. Accept that you may not be able to take on as much at work or home as you previously did. Look at ways to simplify your life and delegate responsibilities to others.

• Set limits with your veteran regarding any out-of-control anger reactions or drug or alcohol use. You don't deserve to be threatened, hurt, or put in harmful situations that jeopardize your safety or the safety of your family. Determine which behaviors you're willing to accept and which you aren't. Setting limits could mean asking your veteran to leave the home for a period of time or to get treatment (such as substance abuse or anger management treatment) in order to stay in the home. Setting limits sends a clear message to your veteran about how much you care about his or her safety, as well as your own.

• Make a commitment with your veteran to help support him or her in using the strategies in this chapter. In most instances, it will be very difficult for your veteran to ask you or anybody for help. Offer to support him or her by doing the exercises in this chapter together. Simply talking about the exercises can be an extremely helpful first step.

• Take care of yourself and get the emotional help *you* need. It's easy to "lose yourself" when your veteran is struggling with his or her adjustment to being home from war. For *you* to be at your best, though, you need to feel energized and ready to go. Make sure you participate in activities that replenish your energy and spirit, like exercise and talking with friends. Get the support you need from family, friends, the community, and medical and mental health professionals so you can then help your veteran.

4

Grief and Loss

Jacob, an Army Reserve medic from St. Louis, Missouri, can't stop wondering if the men and women he triaged lived, or died. At night as he tries to sleep, images of the injured service men and women he tried to save flood his mind. Jacob desperately wishes he knew all their names. Maybe then he could find out if they made it home alive.

As of December 2005, more than 2000 American service men and women have died in the Iraq war. As a returning veteran, when you hear this overwhelming statistic, you may actually see faces of your fellow service men and women. In fact, just thinking about the casualties from this war and the war in Afghanistan may leave you with a whole range of reactions. Maybe you lost a close buddy from training, or a superior you admired. If you're a medic, you may see the faces of fallen service men and women, many unknown. If you're a Casualty Notification Officer working in the States, you may share pangs of loss as you inform families of the deaths of their loved ones in Iraq or Afghanistan. Or perhaps you feel fortunate that you didn't die or witness the death of a fellow veteran, yet you still feel the weight of those who were lost. You may be burdened by visions of civilian dead, such as nationals or foreign aid workers.

For many service men and women, being in the presence of death and dying is a new and overwhelming experience. Besides the loss of those who died, you may feel a personal loss inside yourself—a loss of innocence and trust. Now that you're home, you may wonder if this sense of loss is normal or if the detailed images of death you see and your strong reactions to them are actually a sign of weakness. They're not. Your feelings are typical. As you transition home, it's time to confront your pain and learn to cope with your grief and loss. This chapter is about the thoughts and feelings that people typically experience after a traumatic loss. It answers frequently asked questions about emotional reactions to loss. It also presents strategies for coping with the emotional aftereffects of loss and suggests when it might be appropriate to seek professional help.

What Is Grief?

Grieving is the way that a person responds to a loss. It involves suffering and emotional pain. It can involve a wide range of emotions and apply to a lot of different situations, such as loss of innocence, loss of a close friend, witnessing the loss of life in general, or loss of a physical ability or appendage. In the context of war, loss is generally experienced as sudden and violent. Such traumatic losses may lead to reactions that include shock, despair, anger, guilt, or numbness. These and other intense emotional responses to loss are very common, and if they're not debilitating and don't continue for a long period of time, they shouldn't be cause for concern.

Reactions to Sudden Loss

Christine, a 24-year-old service woman who had returned from Afghanistan was asked how she felt about witnessing the death of a young Afghani child while she was there, she replied, "I felt nothing . . . I knew I should feel sad or surprised or upset, especially because I have my own children back in the U.S., but I didn't. It's as if I had become cold-hearted and unemotional. This death didn't even faze me, and I'm bothered by that."

Common initial reactions to a sudden traumatic loss are varied. They can include:

- Shock
- Disbelief
- Disorientation
- Helplessness
- Despair
- Feeling numb, or disconnected from others

Later reactions commonly experienced within weeks or months of a sudden loss also are diverse. They can include:

- Being unable to get rid of unwanted thoughts about the circumstances of the death
- Having difficulty falling or staying asleep; nightmares
- Having angry outbursts or being frequently irritable
- Feeling numb and detached, or having a hard time feeling close to or intimate with people you love
- Being unable to enjoy your usual activities
- Feeling depressed or hopeless
- Having difficulty concentrating at home or at work or on specific tasks
- Experiencing physical symptoms such as heart pounding, aches and pains, stomach and bowel distress
- Experiencing changes in appetite or eating habits
- Feeling tired or exhausted
- Overusing alcohol, medication, or drugs

NUMBING AND AVOIDANCE

Like many people, you may have felt unfazed and even robotic after you witnessed or heard about a sudden traumatic death during war. This doesn't mean that you didn't care at the time or that you didn't really hear or understand what happened. The pain of the loss simply caused you to go numb or to deny the truth. This initial numbness probably helped you manage your grief so it didn't overwhelm you. During the Vietnam War, a common expression veterans used to help numb out a horrible event they witnessed was *"Don't mean nothing."* In war zones like Iraq and Afghanistan—or Vietnam—it's especially important to stay calm and not let your emotions interfere with your duties. As you focused on surviving the next fire fight or sniper attack and getting back to the base, you didn't have time to process the traumatic death you heard about or watched. You buried your grief in the struggle to survive. It was part of your military training. You were taught that showing emotions was a sign of weakness, so you were discouraged from grieving.

Now that you're home, you may continue to feel emotionally numb or "empty," as you did at war, and you may have a hard time feeling close to loved ones. The numbness you continue to feel was a useful tool for fighting a war, but today you may be hanging onto this numbness to avoid facing the pain of your loss and to protect yourself from being engulfed in sadness. You may fear that if you allow yourself to cry, you will never be able to stop, so you never shed a tear. To make sure the pain doesn't surface, you may turn to alcohol or drugs. It's also common for veterans to return from war and immediately become unusually busy. For example, you may be burying yourself in your work or in an endless number of things that need fixing around the house. Yet emotional numbness may be interfering with your relationships and your ability to enjoy the things that used to bring you pleasure.

ANGER

A natural human emotion, anger may stem from feelings of fear or helplessness, guilt or self-blame, or simply from a sense of outrage and unfairness. It may also be the only way that you know to express intense feelings. Unlike tears, anger is typically a more acceptable form of emotional expression in a military environment, especially in the context of war. But in the context of civilian work or family, frequent expressions of anger are unproductive and potentially harmful.

GUILT

Among those who have experienced a sudden loss, especially veterans returning from a war zone, a common reaction is guilt. The sheer joy and relief of being home may cause you to feel guilty that you're not properly mourning those who died in Iraq or Afghanistan. Or you may feel guilty that your life was spared when others around you died. Perhaps you believe that your life is not as worthwhile as the life of a fellow veteran who was lost. You may believe that you were in some way responsible for the deaths of fellow service men and women because you weren't at your regular assignment at the time they were attacked. It's very common to take on too much responsibility for deaths that you have little to no control over. When you review what happened you'll probably distort the amount of control you had over the situation. Usually this occurs because you now have the luxury of considering all your options in a safe environment and over a long period of time. This feeling of responsibility can compound your sense of guilt. Guilt may also arise from regrets over things you either said or think you should have said, but didn't, before a buddy was killed.

Feelings of guilt may not only cause outbursts of anger, but can also lead to depression. Guilt can cause you to feel insecure and to question your ability to make decisions. It can also lead you to withdraw from relationships because you feel worthless or because you fear that you might let someone down. Guilt can prevent you from seeking help or support when you need it, because you don't believe you deserve to feel better. It's important to remember that feeling better or appreciating being home doesn't mean that you are dishonoring or forgetting those who were lost.

DEPRESSION

For some, normal grieving may turn to intense feelings of emptiness, loneliness, and even depression. This may be accompanied by problems such as fatigue, loss of interest in normal activities, unhealthy changes in eating and sleeping habits, lack of motivation and purpose, and social isolation. At its worst, depression may lead to persistent thoughts of death, dying, or suicide.

Frequently Asked Questions about Grief

HOW LONG DOES GRIEF LAST?

Although the experience of wartime loss never completely fades, grief reactions usually begin to improve within a few weeks to a few months. Gradually, most people find their mood brightening and their activities increasing. This grieving period may not begin, though, until you have returned home and settled back into your relationships and normal routine and you feel it's safe to begin the grieving process. Specific issues that can increase the length of your grieving period or make it more difficult are:

- Previous losses that were similar to your war-zone losses or that were particularly difficult, such as the loss of a sibling or close friend
- Losses that occur soon after your return home, reminding you of your war-zone losses, such as the death of a grandparent or loss of a pet
- Current problems with a spouse, close friend, or family member
- Feelings of guilt or responsibility for the loss

WILL THE GRIEVING BE WORSE AT PARTICULAR TIMES?

You may feel worse when you're in a situation that reminds you of your loss. Reminders may include places, people, feelings, sequences of events, time of day, or news coverage about the war. For example, when you pass cemeteries, you may have flashes of fallen comrades that trigger pangs of emotional pain. It's also common for grieving to intensify around anniversary dates of particular deaths or losses, such as the time a close buddy was killed, the date you returned home after deployment, or the day your unit was mortared and several comrades were seriously injured. Sometimes the reminders may not be obvious, so you may have to think for a while to identify what triggered a strong reaction. Usually you can identify something, but not always.

WHAT IS PREVENTING ME FROM
COPING WITH MY LOSSES?

Unfortunately, many cultural myths or stereotypes we grew up with about grief and loss may be interfering with your ability to readjust to life after war. Here are some myths about grief:

- Grieving means I'm weak.
- If I let myself feel anything about my loss of a friend or loved one, I'll completely lose it or won't be able to function.
- If I feel happiness, I'm disrespecting and deserting my fallen comrades.
- If I move on with my life, I will stop thinking about those I lost.

It's important to recognize when you are having these types of thoughts about grief and loss. Challenge these ideas by telling yourself that they are not truths but myths or stereotypes.

WHAT CAN I DO TO HELP MYSELF?

Coping strategies that are helpful in recovering from a sudden loss are to:

- Get plenty of sleep and eat well.
- Exercise regularly.
- Decrease your use of alcohol and other substances such as coffee and cigarettes. These usually make people feel worse in the long run.
- Pay attention to your body, and don't push yourself too hard.
- Plan leisure activities alone and with friends and family.
- Assume that you'll have lots of different feelings about your loss, and expect these to last for a period of time.
- Write down thoughts and feelings about your loss.
- Recognize that each person grieves differently and that there's not a set amount of time to "recover."
- Think about and prize meaningful lessons you may have gained from your loss. For example, you may have a clearer understanding of what really matters to you in life, such as not taking loved ones for granted.
- Try to not dwell on changing the past. Instead, focus on making the most of the present and the future, which you can change.
- Tell yourself reassuring, kind statements about your loss, like "My buddy is in a safe place now" or "I did the best I could at the time in a very difficult situation."
- Use the Grief Exercises on pages 122 to help you work through your loss and move toward forgiveness. Remember that no one exercise is right for everyone or every situation, so don't be afraid to modify an exercise to make it your own. These exercises are designed to help you grieve, so it's a good idea to do them in a safe, comfortable place where you won't be interrupted.

HOW DO I LEARN TO FORGIVE MYSELF?

> **Louis** is a 58-year-old Vietnam veteran Marine from Providence, Rhode Island, who for 40 years carried with him guilt regarding the death of a young Vietnamese boy whom he mistakenly killed because he thought the boy was going to shoot him. "It took me years to figure out how to forgive myself. I don't want these service men and women from Iraq and Afghanistan to spend that much time suffering. They need to figure out how to forgive themselves so they can move forward."

If a war-zone death occurs and you still feel that you're significantly the cause of someone's death, you may need to work toward self-forgiveness.

After years of struggling with overwhelming guilt, Louis began volunteer work with inner-city children. Not only did he begin to find forgiveness, but he found that he had a natural ability to connect with and help troubled children.

If you indeed made an error that contributed to someone's death, what will *you* need to do to forgive yourself? Some of the grief exercises provided can help you begin to forgive yourself.

SHOULD I TALK TO FAMILY OR FRIENDS ABOUT HOW I'M FEELING?

It's often helpful to talk to friends and family about what happened and how you're feeling. Sharing your grief with people you care about, who did not share your loss directly, can be helpful because they can be supportive without being as personally affected by your loss. But remember that spouses and other family members may not understand your preoccupation with a lost buddy, especially if it's someone whom you knew for a relatively short period of time. Be sure to start by sharing positive memories about your friend, including photographs and mementos of times you had together. Describing the things that you enjoyed and shared with your buddy will help you begin to value your memories instead of only experiencing them as painful.

Text continued on page 124.

GRIEF EXERCISES

Create a Memory Book: Put together a scrapbook of mementos from your friendship with a deceased comrade, or a general memory book to honor those who have died. Include in this scrapbook a page that describes your favorite memories, such as the things you admired and learned from your fellow veterans.

Create a Ritual: Honor the person or people who died while you were in Iraq or Afghanistan in a personal way by creating a ceremony or ritual that you can do to "say goodbye" either once or on a regular basis, such as annually. Some examples of ceremonies or rituals are:

- Think of a place that you know the deceased person enjoyed, such as the beach or a lake, and leave a memento from your relationship there.
- Volunteer to work at an organization that you know was important to the deceased.
- Make a sacred space in your home to commemorate the deceased.
- Donate money to an organization in the name of the deceased.
- Design a piece of art in honor of the deceased, and place it visibly in your home.
- Request thoughts or prayers from those in your community or at your place of worship in honor of the deceased.

Write a Letter to the Deceased: It can be a general letter addressed to all those who were lost, or a specific letter to a fallen buddy or superior. Describe the thoughts and feelings you've had about his or her death. Write about the things you appreciated about him or her and the things you will miss. When you're done, write a letter from your buddy addressed to yourself. Try to write from your friend's perspective, responding as he or she would have. Some people find it helpful to read both letters aloud or share them with a close family member or friend.

Write a Letter to the Loved Ones of the Deceased: You may want the parents, spouse, or children of a fallen veteran to know how important and respected he or she was to you and the troops, or you may want for them to understand the sacrifice and bravery this person displayed at the end of his or her life. Sharing these things through a letter or e-mail can help both you and the veteran's family better manage the grief of your loss. In some instances, visiting with the family members of a fallen buddy may be especially helpful for grieving your loss.

Consider Your Share of Responsibility
This exercise is to help you cope with a war-zone death for which you feel some responsibility. Write down what percent out of 100 you think you are responsible for this death (say, 60 percent). Then ask yourself the following questions:
- What percent of responsibility should the enemy have for this death? Write down what percent you think they were responsible.
- What about other people who were there? Do they share some responsibility for what happened? Write down what percent you think they were responsible.
- What percent of responsibility does our government deserve? Write down what percent you think it was responsible.
- Was the death accidental or intentional? Were you acting under orders?
- Were there other factors involved? Were you tired, hungry, frustrated? Did you recently deal with other traumatic or difficult operations?
- Are there any additional factors you need to consider?

If the person who died was a friend, ask yourself the following questions:
- Would your friend have said that you were responsible for his or her death?
- Would your friend want you to feel guilty for his or her death?
- What kind of a life would he or she want you to have?
- When you take into account all the others involved in this death and all the relevant factors, how much responsibility do you share regarding the incident? Is it less than you had originally thought?

In realistically examining the situation, you'll find that the amount of responsibility you give yourself will decrease. To obtain a more realistic account of your role in the death, complete this exercise a minimum of three times over a one-month period.

WHEN SHOULD I SEEK HELP FOR MY REACTIONS?

Seek help for grief reactions anytime you feel it would be useful. There are no hard and fast rules about when you should get help. For some, seeking help close in time to their loss may be beneficial, especially if they don't have others to talk to or are having a very strong reaction. Others may wish to see if the distress lessens with time. As a rule of thumb, consider talking to a professional if:

- Three to six months have gone by and you don't feel that things have improved greatly.
- Your reactions to loss seem out of control (say you have suicidal thoughts).
- The way you're feeling is interfering with your ability to work, spend time with family and friends, or perform household responsibilities.

WHAT KIND OF HELP SHOULD I GET?

Some veterans returning from war choose to seek help from spiritual leaders in their communities, such as ministers, priests, or rabbis. Or you may feel more comfortable going to someone who is trained in helping people with emotional problems, such as a psychologist, social worker, psychiatrist, or marriage and family therapist. These professionals can be found through employee assistance programs at your workplace, in community mental health centers, at your nearest VA hospital or Veterans Readjustment Counseling Center, or in private practice. Mental health professionals are trained to talk with people about grief and loss to help them understand their reactions and cope better. Psychiatrists are also trained in prescribing medications that may help with some grief reactions, such as troubled sleep or depression. You can get professional help with grief and loss in the form of individual, couples, family, or group therapy.

TIPS FOR PARTNERS, FAMILY MEMBERS, AND FRIENDS

Sam came home from the war unsure if he could talk to anyone about seeing his good friend killed in Iraq. His father, a Vietnam veteran, was able to help Sam by sharing some of the losses he experienced in Vietnam and his initial difficulties in dealing with them when he returned home. This talk helped Sam work through his grief while making his dad feel good that he was able to use his own experience to help his son. Sam and his dad got closer because of this discussion.

Your loved one has returned home from the war and is having strong grief reactions from his or her combat experience. Avoiding talking about this experience is a fairly common response. Sometimes a veteran will need help dealing with grief and loss. Here are tips for you to help him or her begin talking about wartime loss.

Bring up the issue of loss with your veteran.

Directly ask if he or she is feeling bad about any death from war or combat. If you've served in previous wars or faced the death of loved ones before, you can help your veteran feel that what he or she is going through is "normal" by disclosing a small piece of your experience. Remember to do this only if you're comfortable discussing your own loss. The goal is to use your own experience as an icebreaker to get your veteran to discuss his or her experience. Recognize that even if you've never been exposed to combat or war, you can still talk about how typical it is to have strong reactions to the death of loved ones or friends. Refer to the grief reactions given in this chapter and then ask a question like "Did you have this experience?"

Ask your veteran how you can best help.

The process of talking about the loss of a comrade may take some time. At first your veteran may not be interested in sharing with you, but don't give up. You can let him or her know that you will be ready to talk when the time is right. He or she may want to grieve alone. Respect this choice and discuss how you can help provide a safe place where he or she can grieve without interruption. On the other hand, if he or she begins to talk, try not to be overwhelmed by or judgmental about what you hear. Instead, try to listen without reacting. Show that you understand what he or she is going through. You can also ask if he or she would like to jointly do one of the exercises mentioned above. For example, you can help with the memory book exercise by asking questions about the deceased person: "What was he or she like?" "What would be good pictures to put in a memory book?" Or you can help your returning veteran create a ritual to honor the deceased. Doing these types of exercises or rituals together can bring you closer to one another.

Sometimes a more subtle approach, like leaving material about grief or loss in a place where he or she is apt to read it, can be a good strategy to start with. For instance, leave this section of the book in a place where your returning veteran can see it.

Encourage your veteran to seek professional help if necessary.

If you're concerned that he or she is depressed or seriously troubled by grief and loss from war, urge him or her to see a mental health professional. For example, you can contact the local VA hospital or Veterans Readjustment Counseling Center for help.

5

Changed Views of Self, Others, and the World

Paul, a 38-year-old reservist from Charleston, South Carolina, believes that he is a different person since going to Iraq. Before deployment, he saw himself as carefree and sociable. He dreamed of a bright future for himself and his family. Now, disillusioned by war, he can't trust people. He doesn't plan for the future. His wife describes him as cold and bitter toward people and the world—yes, even toward their dog. Nothing seems to matter anymore.

Since losing her leg to a rocket-propelled grenade in Iraq, **Yolanda**, a 23-year-old Marine from Buffalo, New York, sees herself as a disabled person with no future. She used to feel confident and strong. She was proud to have served in combat. But today, she doubts herself and her abilities. She believes she is defective and weak. This negative view of herself is a lot different from the positive view she had at war, when she felt useful and even powerful.

Ron, a successful 59-year-old businessman and Vietnam Army veteran from Albuquerque, New Mexico, was recently discussing his war experience. "It was the hardest thing I've ever done. There is nothing that compares to having to deal with the insanity and chaos of war. When you're over there, you end up getting close to other guys, especially when you're being fired at. You learn about what it means to really have to depend on people you would never have known if it wasn't for the war.

When I first returned from Vietnam, my sleep and anger were really giving me problems. I felt like I had wasted a year of my life and had lost myself in the process. At first I tried to deal with it by drinking, but fortunately I woke up and got help for myself and my family. I now look back on my service with a lot of pride. Because of my war experience, I know how to get along with almost anybody. It also taught me how to keep my work in perspective. I mean, I can have a bad day at the office, but no one dies. I think when you've seen a lot of death and maybe come close to death yourself, you learn to appreciate life in a new way."

Serving in a war can affect you deeply and in many different ways. After returning home, you may feel like you have lost your direction in life or that you have gotten off course. Maybe you feel as if you have lost a big part of yourself. Like Paul, some of you may feel completely changed by war. Even though you weren't physically injured, you feel that some part of yourself has been wounded. For those of you who were injured at war like Yolanda, your body has changed in ways that you may never have imagined possible. Physical injuries from war may include lost limbs, lost eyesight, impaired hearing, traumatic brain injury (covered later in this chapter), an amputation, a shattered knee, shrapnel wounds, burns, pain, and many other types of physical problems or losses in physical abilities. With physical injuries like these come all kinds of changes—not only in what you can do but also in how you identify yourself and look at life in general. Whatever image you had of yourself before Iraq or Afghanistan, it didn't include the physical limitations you now face.

No matter what type of challenges or losses you faced in Iraq or Afghanistan, it is common for views about yourself, family, others, community, and life itself to change afterward. Your views may have been slightly altered or been totally transformed. For some veterans of Iraq and Afghanistan, war has turned their views about many things upside down. You may discover that people, places, and things that used to be important just aren't anymore. You may find that you can't imagine a future for yourself. Maybe you joined the Reserves to get an education, but now that you've returned, you think school is a waste of time. If you went into the military to escape family problems, your war experiences may have confirmed your worst fears about life. The escape you were looking for backfired, and now you regret entering the military. Serving in a war can also shake or even destroy your faith in the government, the military, other people, or a higher power.

At the same time, in an odd way, fighting in Iraq or Afghanistan may have brought a more positive view of life. You may value family and friends more, take advantage of the moment more, or appreciate the freedoms of the United States more. Like Ron, you may have initially returned with problems and bitterness, but in time you too can develop an appreciation for your war experience and the things you learned from it. Maybe war confirmed the importance of your spiritual beliefs or bolstered your faith.

This chapter invites you to take a look at how your views have changed because of your deployment in Iraq or Afghanistan. It asks whether you see yourself, others, and the world differently since war and, if so, how these changes are affecting you. Strategies are offered to help you deal with changed views if you feel that they're getting in the way of your readjustment to life at home.

Safety and Trust

Your ability to feel safe and to trust in yourself, other people, and the world may have shifted because of war. For instance, your training and experience in combat may have led you to fear that you'll become violent if you feel threatened in public. You can't trust yourself, you think, so you don't go out. If you have a physical injury from war, you may now feel weak and think that you won't be able to protect yourself from harm like you used to.

Before deployment, you probably trusted people around you, like those at work or in your neighborhood. But today when you go outside, you may be extra cautious, even suspicious, of people and your surroundings, unsure whom you can trust and what's safe. In the chaos and unpredictability of war, you probably learned not to trust anything or anybody except your buddies. You were unsure of who the enemy was and who your ally was. You may also have been trained to perform one type of duty but ended up doing something completely different. You had a lot of things to fear. It's been hard for you to make sense of much of what you experienced. Now that you're home, you still feel the effects of war and the way it has shaken your sense of yourself and the world. No *wonder* you still think you're unsafe and can't trust people. You still feel exposed and vulnerable, as if the enemy could attack you or your loved ones at any time.

Common views that veterans returning from Iraq and Afghanistan have about safety and trust include:

The world isn't a safe place anymore.

I can't trust anybody, not even myself.

The government betrayed me.

Others want to harm me.

I must be ready for danger at all times.

Nobody keeps their promises.

Control and Power

You may notice changes in the way you think about control and power since fighting in a war. You may think that nothing you do will make a difference in your life or other people's lives, so you feel weak and powerless. Whatever you do, it's as if your hands are tied behind your back or you are in quicksand. Although you may have done what was expected of you in war, you found out that you couldn't personally control the outcome of the war or what happened next. IEDs, sniper attacks, physical injuries, deaths, and all kinds of chaotic events were beyond your control no matter how hard you tried to stop them. Since you've returned home, it's natural to feel that you can't control what happens to you or your loved ones, as if you are still at war. You believe that you're helpless and can't take charge of your life. In turn, you may give up on trying to do things that would improve your situation or make you feel better. Or you may do just the opposite. You may work extra hard to control every little thing in your life, or try desperately to control and protect loved ones to the point of being overprotective.

At the same time, some veterans come to possess a sense of indestructibility. This "invincibility" may drive them to do whatever they want after they come home, even if it's dangerous or reckless. And some may believe they have power over others, as though they were back in the military running a unit. Or maybe you're one of those who think they don't have to listen to authority figures anymore, since those in command weren't able to stop bad things from happening during the war.

Common views that veterans returning from Iraq and Afghanistan have about control and power include:

I can't control anything in my life.

Nothing I do will make a difference, so why should I try?

I'm trapped—there's no way out.

The only way to protect my family is to make them follow my orders.

I've got special power and clout because I went to war.

I'm indestructible.

Future Outlook

Your beliefs about planning for the future may also have shifted because of war. Before you left for Iraq or Afghanistan, maybe you were one of those people who made plans months in advance, had big dreams for yourself and your family, and pictured growing old after a life filled with accomplishments. You may have envisioned a long career in the military. But now you may struggle with setting short- and long-term goals, seeing a future, wanting to stay in the military, or even being associated with the military at all.

Difficulty in planning for the future can stem from the time when you were deployed and had to live day-by-day without knowing if you'd live or die. Survival in the moment, the hour, the day, the evening—that was all that mattered. Now you may be surprised that you survived the war, and even more shocked to actually be reunited with your family. You come home with a "short-timer" view; you're still living day-to-day and not setting goals too far off in the future.

Confusing this picture is the possibility that you may be redeployed to Iraq or Afghanistan. How can you seriously think about future plans, like buying a home, marrying, going to school, or starting your own business, if you don't know whether you'll be sent to war again? And if you are redeployed, you don't know if you'll be given a second chance to make it home alive again. Redeployment anxiety is discussed on page 134.

Common views that veterans returning from Iraq and Afghanistan have about planning for the future include:

It's not worth my time and energy to plan for the future because I may be redeployed.

What's the point of trying today when it all can blow up in my face?

I never think beyond today, much less tomorrow or the next day.

I won't live much longer.

My dreams for the future are gone.

Self-Worth and Self-Esteem

War often pollutes beliefs about human worth and value, along with dreams about the future. You may think you're weak or cowardly because you felt intense fear or terror at times during the war. You may feel ashamed for having been so scared. These feelings go against your military training and society's expectations that military personnel should be strong and fearless. Besides, you may think you're weak for asking others for help now that you're home. You may wonder what's wrong with you that you are so affected by the war. You may feel like "damaged goods," doubting yourself and your abilities, no longer believing you can rely on yourself. You may think that you could have done more to help others who served with you, beating yourself up for not having acted more quickly, panicking, or making one decision instead of another. It seems to make no sense that you survived while others didn't.

For some veterans, changed views like these strongly affect the core of their identity. They describe themselves as monsters or animals when they relate things they did in combat. Although at the time they were following orders, they blame themselves for any suffering that occurred as a result of performing their duties. They come to feel ugly about who they are, and disgusted with themselves inside and out. They may think they don't deserve to have survived, let alone to be happy now that they've returned home. Veterans with physical injuries from war may see themselves as broken or inadequate human beings because of their disability. You may relate to these ideas even if you weren't injured. Maybe you think you're a violent, bad, or unlovable person because you harmed or killed people while in combat or because you saw such awful things, like burned or dismembered bodies or the corpses of children. Judging yourself negatively because of things you did or saw while at war can lead to deep feelings of shame and loss, and it can change your sense of who you are.

Text continued on page 136.

REDEPLOYMENT ANXIETY

For some veterans, redeployment to Iraq or Afghanistan may seem appealing because it seems to offer the possibility of meaning, excitement, camaraderie, patriotism, and respect—things you may not find at home right now. For others, though, the mere thought of redeployment may fuel anxiety and nervousness. "Redeployment anxiety" can bring on emotional stress—edginess, anger, helplessness, fear, hopelessness, resentment, and confusion—when you picture being called to return to Iraq or Afghanistan. Negative thoughts and images of the war, upsetting dreams about redeployment, and worst-case scenarios may haunt you. Redeployment anxiety can also cause physical stress, including such symptoms as fatigue, sleeplessness, a changed appetite, muscle tension, and headaches. In fact, symptoms of redeployment anxiety may be affecting your entire family.

Uncertainty about redeployment—questions about whether, when, for how long, and in what capacity you'll be deployed this time—can put you and those you care about in a state of limbo. You may find yourself torn between readjusting to civilian life and staying in combat mode. This tug-of-war can create tension, as you're pulled by loved ones to return to a "normal" life with them while drawn toward those still in Iraq and Afghanistan to be ready to stand by them again.

Redeployment anxiety is understandable and normal. Many veterans returning from Iraq and Afghanistan express such concerns. For National Guard and Reserve returnees in particular, the possibility of redeployment is a reality, and few options exist to prevent it. Some active duty military returnees, on being told they'll be sent back to Iraq or Afghanistan, instead choose to get out of the service altogether.

It's no wonder you may not want to talk with your loved ones about the possibility of redeployment. You don't want to worry them, and there may be no realistic way to stop it. Yet your loved ones are probably worrying in silence too. They worry about being separated from you again, and maybe even fear you won't come back at all. The risk of redeployment is like the elephant in the living room that nobody talks about.

Here are tips to help you deal with redeployment anxiety:

- *Communicate to your loved ones your fears about possible redeployment.* Listen to their feelings and concerns about possibly being separated again. Try to be open and understanding with one another. Strive not to become defensive or angry.
- *Keep in mind that your anxiety is reasonable.* It's very hard to fully readjust to home, knowing that your risk of redeployment is high.
- *Avoid keeping secrets from loved ones about your redeployment schedule.* Share any information you have about your next assignment so they're not surprised.
- *Talk to other military service men and women in similar situations.* It will help you feel less alone in handling your redeployment anxiety.
- *Encourage your family to talk with other military families.* This can be a way of obtaining mutual support and helping them know they're not alone.
- *Speak to a therapist or counselor about your redeployment anxiety.* Invite loved ones to join you so you all can talk about this sensitive topic.
- *Be prepared for redeployment.* Line up support for your loved ones in advance, from folks in your neighborhood and community, in case you're called up on short notice.
- *Consider all options regarding your contract of service with the military.* What would happen if you left the military earlier than planned? Could you be transferred to a unit that's less likely to be redeployed? Make a list of pros and cons of these options, and talk them over with your loved ones.
- *Get help from military and civilian doctors and the VA.* If you don't want to be redeployed and think you have a significant war-related disability, seek help from military and nonmilitary doctors and VA clinicians and personnel. Get these professionals' support by having them document the extent of your disability in writing. This information may be used to help determine your fitness for duty.
- *Write your US senators and representative to express your concerns and perspectives on redeployment.* As part of their constituency, they're there to serve you and represent your interests.

Common views that veterans returning from Iraq and Afghanistan have about their self-worth and self-esteem include:

I don't deserve love from my family anymore.

I'm incompetent because I didn't save my buddies.

I failed at war.

I am a bad person for the things I did at war.

I'm not worthy of anybody's care.

I'm weak for asking for help.

I'm useless, now that I have a physical disability.

If I told you what I did when I served, you would hate me.

Relationships and Closeness

War may have changed not only the views you have about your own worth but also how you think and feel about being with other people, including your family and close friends. Since returning from war, you may feel extremely out of place, alienated, or strange, even in your own home. Some veterans from Iraq and Afghanistan say they feel like loners or misfits in society, as if nobody can understand them unless they have served in the military. You may feel this way too. You may believe that the only people you can talk to or hang out with are those you drill with on weekends, or buddies you served with.

Now that you're home, it may seem like you can't feel emotions such as love, compassion, or understanding for other people, even family members and friends with whom you were close before war. Maybe you feel hardened, cold, and bitter, as if a part of yourself—your "nice side" or "good part"—has died.

You may fear that family, friends, or others will abandon you the same way your war experience may have left you feeling abandoned by the military, the government, or fellow soldiers who died. So you avoid people most of the time and want to be left alone. All these thoughts and feelings can make it hard to be comfortable with people, including your family. You may even have developed the belief that you can't or shouldn't be close with others.

Common views that veterans returning from Iraq and Afghanistan have about relationships and closeness include:

I can't relate to my civilian friends anymore.

I'd rather be by myself than with my family.

I feel like an outsider even in my own home.

I think something is wrong with me because I don't have any feelings for people I used to care for.

Others will die on me like my military friends, so why should I bother getting close?

Meaning and Purpose of Life

Beliefs about what is meaningful and worthwhile in your life may have been corroded as a result of war. At the time, serving with buddies on a common mission probably brought a strong sense of purpose and honor. It felt good to be relied on and needed by others in your unit. The loyalty that developed between you and your buddies may have been stronger than you could ever have imagined. This allegiance may be deeper today than what you feel toward your family and civilian friends.

Besides this loyalty, you probably were given a lot of responsibility when you were at war, and chances are you shouldered it quite well. Real satisfaction, or even a "high," may have come from taking on this responsibility—maybe the most responsibility you ever had in a job. Then too, the idea of serving your country may have given you a sense of purpose that you've been unable to achieve in your civilian job. At times, you may have felt powerful and invincible, such as when you escaped from a burning Humvee, saved a friend, or rescued an Iraqi child. Today, back home, you may miss the sense of responsibility and satisfaction you got from war. Although you may not want to admit it, you may feel that nothing in civilian life compares to the excitement and "high" you got in the military as a patriotic service member and loyal comrade. And if you received physical injuries from the war, you may long for the fulfillment and pride you got from serving before you were hurt.

Common views that veterans returning from Iraq and Afghanistan have about meaning and purpose in their lives include:

Nothing matters, now that I'm home.

My responsibilities here are nothing compared to those I had in the military.

I don't have any purpose or motivation for living.

I'm not sure the war was worth it.

What is going on here in the US is trivial compared to what's going on in Iraq.

The only satisfaction I get these days is following the news so I can hear how my buddies are doing.

Civilian life is boring and meaningless.

Spirituality and Faith

War challenges some people's spiritual beliefs. You may question why your higher power (if you believe in one) would allow such awful, pointless events to happen. You may think your supreme being failed you, abandoning you at the very time you needed comfort and guidance most. You may believe that the spiritual force you were raised to have faith in no longer protects you. You may not think you deserve divine protection because of the acts of violence or destruction you were a part of in war. Maybe you've come to doubt the existence of a higher power altogether.

Common beliefs that veterans returning from Iraq or Afghanistan have about spirituality and faith include:

I no longer have faith that God exists.

My higher power betrayed me.
I'm too bad to be loved by a higher power.
How could there be a God, given what I've seen?
God can't protect anybody.
God isn't fair.

Positive Change

Ron, whom you met at the beginning of this chapter, returned from Vietnam feeling angry and lost, but with time he managed to find something positive—you might even say *wisdom*—from his war experience. The positive changes that Ron experienced, and that you can too, can only come from struggling and coping with a traumatic event like war. "Posttraumatic growth" is not an uncommon experience for war veterans. For some, it means seeing themselves as more self-reliant or capable. For others, it means appreciating friends and family more deeply. Still others say that after returning home from war, the struggle of coping with a physical disability or emotional problems made them take a serious look at their priorities and values. In almost every case, posttraumatic growth means change. First, you have to change the way you see yourself and your war experience, and then you have to incorporate those changes into your daily life. Here are practical tips for understanding and accepting the problematic views that you may have developed as a result of the war and then going on to use your war experience to make positive changes in your life and the lives of others.

Coping with Changed Views

After reading this chapter, you may want to copy the Changed Views Chart on page 140 onto a piece of paper and fill out the different sections. For example, write down what your views were about safety and trust before going to war, what they are

CHANGED VIEWS CHART

Views about yourself, others, and the world	What were your views before going to war?	What are your views after going to war?	How are your views affecting you today?	New Views (when you identify an "extreme view," replace it with a less extreme view here)
Safety and Trust				
Control and Power				
Future Outlook				
Self-Worth and Self-Esteem				
Relationships and Closeness				
Meaning and Purpose in Life				
Spirituality and Faith				

since the war, and how they are affecting your readjustment at home. Do this for each topic (safety and trust, control and power, future outlook, and so on). Leave the column labeled *New Views* blank for now.

Now that you've completed the chart, follow the strategies below:

Review your past and current views in each of the different areas. Notice where and how your views have changed since going to war. Give yourself time to think about these changes.

Be aware that it's normal for your views to have changed. In life, we go through all kinds of experiences and phases that have an effect on the way we think about ourselves, other people, and the world. Life is always changing, and so are we—not only physically and emotionally, but also in the way we think about and interpret situations. War is an extraordinary event. It makes sense that it can lead you to think differently about life. It's also natural for feelings of loss and sadness to accompany these changed views.

Accept that you and the way you see the world may have changed. You're not the same person you were before you went to war. Who would be? How could you be? None of us is the same person we were a year or two ago, and add to that fighting in a war zone. Accept that it is okay that you and your perspectives have changed. Don't beat yourself up about these changes.

Acceptance is something you have to practice when approaching major life events. For instance, if a person learns he or she can't have children because of war injuries, at first he or she may be upset when seeing friends and family who have children. It's next to impossible to just accept this reality and move on. If you find yourself in this situation, you need to set aside time to mourn what you can't have before you can move toward acceptance.

Text continued on page 144.

TRAUMATIC BRAIN INJURY

What is Traumatic Brain Injury (TBI)?

Traumatic brain injury (TBI) refers to a jolt to the head that disrupts brain function. TBI is an occupational risk for those in the military, afflicting an estimated 15 percent of surviving combat casualties. Men and women serving in Iraq and Afghanistan are at even higher risk for TBI because of recent changes in weaponry and protective gear. Increased usage of IEDs in Operation Iraqi Freedom and Operation Enduring Freedom has led to more blast injuries, and technological advances in helmets and body armor mean that many military personnel are surviving incidents that would have killed them in the past, and are left to live with the aftermath of such physical trauma.

TBI can result from any major blow to the body or head, whether or not the person loses consciousness, is struck directly on the head, or shows any visible sign of injury. Simply absorbing the force of a serious impact is enough to cause bleeding, bruising, or tearing of brain tissue. The brain is encased in bone, so once injuries are sustained, the skull can't expand to contain swelling or bleeding. Even small amounts of pressure on brain tissue can cause problems that may show up either immediately or over time.

What are the effects of TBI?

Because the brain is in some way responsible for every area of functioning, TBI can lead to a wide variety of problems. Physical symptoms such as recurrent headaches, sleep disturbance, and problems with coordination may appear. Cognitive changes are also very common. Survivors of TBI often report that their long-term memory seems as good as ever, but their short-term memory is much worse. Survivors of TBI can have extreme difficulty taking in new information and retrieving it when needed. They can also have problems with attention, concentration, and organizing information. TBI often causes changes in personality, emotional functioning, and ability to relate to others. Survivors may find themselves more prone to strong, unexplained feelings of sadness and anger and may have difficulty communicating their experience to others.

How is TBI diagnosed?

No foolproof medical test exists for detecting TBI. Even advanced brain-imaging techniques such as CT scans and MRIs may not detect major changes in brain structure. The best way of diagnosing TBI is through neuropsychological testing. A specialist asks the survivor a number of questions and has him or her complete tasks that require a range of skills. Studying the survivor's response pattern can yield a better understanding of the nature and extent of his or her problems.

How is TBI treated?

TBI can cause problems in different areas of functioning, so more than one treatment approach often is needed. Treatments can include physical, cognitive, and emotional rehabilitation. A physical therapist's job is to treat impairment in body movement and control, as well as neck and back pain. Cognitive and emotional problems can be addressed in different ways: A speech therapist works at rebuilding language, memory, and social skills, while a counselor or therapist can help improve behavioral control and emotional coping. Finally, psychiatric medication, prescribed by either a psychiatrist or a general physician, can help with symptoms like sleep disturbance and depression.

How can I cope if I or someone I love has suffered TBI?

Coping with the effects of TBI is challenging for the survivor and for everyone in his or her life. Rehabilitation can take a long time. Don't expect rapid improvement. Some problems may respond to treatment right away, but others will require more patience. When possible, emphasize areas of functioning that have not been impaired. Be honest about areas of impairment, and stay open to trying new ways of doing things. Look at websites and books about living with TBI.

Unlike a broken leg in a cast, with TBI there is no readily visible sign that recovery from an injury is taking place, so it's essential to talk openly and directly about the effects of TBI. The survivor should try to explain how he or she is doing and ask for help when

(Text continued on page 144.)

needed, whether from family and friends, a support group, or a counselor or therapist.

Remember that TBI can seriously affect emotional functioning. Survivors report that despite their best efforts, they sometimes cry for no apparent reason, feel easily overwhelmed, and become extremely angry in an instant. Don't get down on yourself about these problems, but recognize that they're symptoms of TBI. Cognitive and emotional rehabilitation—individual therapy, coping skills groups, and anger management training—can help survivors better manage these responses and their effects on relationships with others. Individual therapy and coping groups for loved ones of TBI survivors can also be very helpful.

A thorough neuropsychological assessment will aid you in determining whether you're ready to return to school or work and to identify areas in which you may require extra help. Adjusting to the aftereffects of TBI takes patience, courage, and hope. Every survivor is different, and there's no good way of determining how long it will take to recover or how complete the recovery will be. Whatever the length of the journey, try to stay connected with others, keep your focus on the positives, and, above all, treat yourself with the respect and compassion that you deserve.

In beginning to accept changes you've gone through, it may help to follow the message given in the "Serenity Prayer" (by Reinhold Niebuhr), often used by Alcoholics Anonymous: *God grant me the serenity to accept the things I cannot change; courage to change things I can; and wisdom to know the difference.*

Following the message of this prayer isn't easy. But by accepting that certain changes have occurred in your outlook on life, you can set more realistic expectations for yourself and others. Try to focus on what you *can* change and let be what you *can't* change. Set goals that fit your current situation, not your past situation before deployment. Acceptance means understanding what your shortcomings may be since serving in a war, yet still seeing yourself as a whole and valuable person with a bright future, even though it may not be the one you expected. If you have a physical disability, for example, accept the injury as a part of who you are without letting it *define* who you are.

Identify extreme views you may have today that are causing you stress. Once you've identified these views, try to replace them with a more reasonable perspective. It's important to accept that your outlook on life may be colored by war. Changes in the way you look at the world because of your war experience are very real and to be expected. But review your responses in the Changed Views Chart and notice if any of the views you hold since going to war are extreme. Here, "extreme" means they're not rational, reasonable, or understandable. For instance, in the row about your views on safety and trust since going to war, you may have written "I can't trust anybody anymore." Ask yourself how true this perspective really is. If you actually stop to think about it, maybe there is a person—or even two—whom you can trust.

Extreme views like "I can't trust anybody anymore" are sometimes called "distorted thinking." This type of thinking is not helpful because it can lead to further negative thoughts and feelings. So if you have identified extreme views through this exercise, ask yourself if they're contributing to stressful emotions, such as anxiety or depression, or whether they're making your adjustment home more difficult. If they are, try this strategy:

1. **Identify your distorted thinking.** Below are different types of distorted thinking that many people, including veterans from Iraq and Afghanistan, can get caught up in. See if you might have views that fall into any of these categories.

- *Black-or-White Thinking:* Viewing your military experience in extremes and not seeing anything in between; seeing situations as either good or bad, black or white, all or none, perfect or imperfect. Example: "I completely failed all the men and women in my unit when I left Iraq."

- *Doomsday Thinking:* Viewing your future as hopeless from every angle; thinking that bad outcomes are your destiny no matter what you do. Example: "I will never be able to relate to civilians after serving in war no matter how much I try."

- *Mind-Reading Thinking:* Thinking that other people have negative views about you or negative intentions toward you without any real reason or evidence to support this belief. Example: "Everybody thinks I'm incompetent since I came home from the war."

- *If Only Thinking:* Thinking about the past with regret and disappointment by wondering "If only I had . . . " over and over again. Example: "If only I had waited five more minutes, the convoy wouldn't have been hit by an IED."

2. **Replace the distorted thinking with a more helpful, reasonable view.** For example, you might replace the view "I can't trust anybody anymore" with "It's hard to trust people after going to war, but I do have a few friends I can rely on." On the Changed Views Chart, write this *New View* in the last column across from the view that you're replacing.

3. **Practice saying this new view to yourself so your mind begins to believe in it more strongly.** It takes time and repetition, but after a while you'll begin to believe this new view more and more.

Identify positive views as well as negative ones. Go over your responses on the Changed Views Chart to help shed light on any positive ways your views have been transformed by war. For instance, you may feel thankful to be reunited with your family. You may value time with your family now. Maybe you realize that certain material things aren't as important anymore or that it's important to live each day fully. You may feel grateful to have a job. Or you may appreciate what it means to be in a free country.

Think about what lessons you learned from your war experience that have affected you in a positive way, and ask yourself how you can build on those lessons today.

Find positive meaning in your life today. Think about the things you do daily that give meaning and purpose to your life. You may provide for your family or care for your children. Maybe you've looked after a sick friend or family member or helped a neighbor fix his or her car. Your work may provide a service or create or sell a product that improves people's lives. Or maybe you volunteer once a month at your church or a local community agency. While these day-to-day contributions may not seem as important as the duties you fulfilled at war, they're not without meaning or purpose. As a civilian, too, you can be proud of who you are and the things you're doing to support your community and country. All it takes is to become more aware of the contributions you're making right here at home, whether they're big or small.

Rebuild spiritual beliefs. If after completing the Changed Views Chart you discover that you want to strengthen your spiritual life now that you're home, here are some specific suggestions:

- Find others with similar spiritual beliefs whom you can talk to about your daily struggles and ways to discover more meaning in your civilian life. They may include your partner, family members, or friends.

- Build a sense of community with other people by joining a spiritual organization, becoming involved in your community, or volunteering for a charitable cause. You may want to include your partner, family members, or friends in these activities.

- Set spiritual goals for yourself, like participating in classes or lectures.

TIPS FOR PARTNERS, FAMILY MEMBERS, AND FRIENDS

Not only veterans, but also the families and friends to whom they return, face changes in their views when their veterans return home. Family members and friends who have eagerly awaited the safe return of their veteran may quickly see their expectations shattered. They may discover that their veteran seems greatly different from before he or she left. Their veteran may not be able to do things with them like before. He or she may seem less easygoing, not interested in them, angry, or distant. Family members and friends may blame themselves for these changes. They may experience loss and grieving over the veteran they knew and the dreams they used to share about the future. They may feel like the world they knew with their veteran has vanished.

In addition, family members and friends may have changed the way they view themselves since the time of their veteran's deployment. Maybe a wife who was left with the sole responsibility of caring for the house and children now sees herself as stronger and more independent than before. Or a husband may be bitter and "angry at God and the world" because his partner has been deployed for a second tour. It's normal for family members' and friends' views to shift in all sorts of ways after a loved one goes to war. Here are some suggestions to help family members and friends cope with the changes that have occurred in both their views and the views of their returning veterans.

Be reassuring and patient about changes. Remind your veteran that changes in the way he or she views things or changes in physical abilities are only a part—not all—of who he or she is today. Help him or her begin to accept that certain changes have happened, and that it's okay. Reassure your veteran that you still love him or her and that you plan to support him or her all the way. Although he or she may seem very different since returning from war, keep in mind that not all these changes will be permanent. In time, your veteran may learn to trust again and will probably become more hopeful about the future. The distance that you feel now will likely fade as your veteran becomes more confident in the stability of family and friendships. If your veteran has returned with an injury or disability, he or she may adapt in time to the changes in his or her appearance or ability. Accept that your veteran has been through a life-changing experience, and be patient. Allow your veteran time to reflect on the meaning of his or her war experience.

Likewise, be patient with yourself. Remind yourself that things are likely to change as time goes on. Notice small accomplishments, like how you handle stressful situations or when you and your veteran are able to work together.

Chart the changes. Like your veteran, you may find it helpful to copy the Changed Views Chart in this chapter on to a piece of paper and complete sections of it that you can relate to. You can use this exercise to discover how your views may have changed between the time your veteran went to war and his or her return. Get help from your veteran in completing your chart. This allows him or her to be helpful and supportive to you. It also helps the veteran incorporate what he or she is learning from this chapter.

Help challenge "distorted thinking." Talk with one another about the ideas discussed in this chapter and your thoughts and beliefs about the war. Share how your views have changed and how they're affecting you in such areas as your relationship, visions of the future, and spiritual beliefs. You also may want to challenge each other's views if they seem extreme or distorted. Just hearing such thoughts and beliefs repeated by someone else will help you and your veteran see them from a different perspective. Even the most extreme beliefs can lose their power when they're shared. This joint work becomes a win-win situation for both of you!

Get reacquainted. If the experience of deployment and war has changed you or your veteran in significant ways, you may now feel that you're living with a stranger. Get to know each other again, with the understanding that neither of you may be exactly the same person you were when you first met. Set aside a date night to get reacquainted. You may need to review your basic values and priorities if they've changed for one or both of you since your veteran's deployment.

Maintain realistic hope. Have hope about the future, but don't set your sights on goals that are unrealistic. Having no hope can lead you and your veteran to become demoralized. Set short-term achievable goals for you, your veteran, and your family. Regularly review the progress of these goals. Ask yourself honestly whether the goals are too lofty or not lofty enough, and adjust them accordingly.

6

Returning to Civilian Life

Returning home from war can cause culture shock, leaving you overwhelmed and filled with mixed feelings. At first you may be thrilled to be home and proud about your service, yet you may also feel guilty about leaving your comrades behind. Getting what you need—whether it's taking a shower, seeing your family and friends, having the food you like, or even getting some privacy—is a welcomed change. The sense of freedom you receive on your return to civilian life may be liberating and reassuring. But, over time, not having the order, structure, and discipline that you got used to in the military may feel threatening, foreign, or uncomfortable.

While your choices may have increased now that you're home, this stateside freedom brings with it a special kind of stress. Fitting back into the workplace, classroom, or community can be more anxiety-provoking than you expected. When you were fighting a war, following rules and obeying orders helped keep you and your buddies alive, creating a sense of safety. Without this same type of rigid structure at work, school, or in your neighborhood, you may feel unsafe. You also may become frustrated with colleagues, classmates, or individuals in the community who show disrespect for authority and discipline. On the other hand, you might find some rules imposed on you as a civilian, such as smoking restrictions at work, petty or just plain ludicrous.

This chapter looks at common challenges veterans face in returning to civilian life, such as adjusting to work, school, and community, and offers some solutions to those challenges. It also provides tips to pass along to your civilian employer so they can help you better transition back to the workforce.

Readjusting to Work

José, a member of the National Guard from Phoenix, has returned to his job in the federal government. Although at first he is welcomed back to work, he soon realizes that the old, comfortable position he left now feels awkward and different. José is unclear about his new responsibilities on the job. His supervisor, who did not work with him before his deployment, is unsure how to approach him about his new responsibilities and his experiences in the service.

Returning to work after deployment is an incredibly stressful experience. While some people can make a smooth return to their previous employment, most find this experience challenging.

Employers have had to adapt to your absence. Like your family, they have had to depend on others to perform your former job duties. Your employer most likely was able to accomplish these tasks while you were away by finding new ways to get the job done. He or she may be more comfortable with this new system than the old way things were done when you were last there. Now you face the major hurdle of how to fit into your "new" work environment. Here are a few suggestions for getting over this hurdle. How useful they are will depend on the specifics of your job situation.

TIPS FOR RETURNING TO WORK

Find the right person to speak with before starting work. Learn what has changed at your workplace. In some work environments, discussing the transition back with a union representative (if applicable) may be extremely helpful. In other environments, a friend at work will give you the best information. At still other jobs, your supervisor or a representative from human resources will be the right person to speak with. Whoever you speak with, ask questions about changes that have occurred in your absence. What's different in the work environment? What's the same? How will your specific job be different? How will it be the same? What roles have shifted, what positions have been overhauled, how have the economy and war affected morale? In some situations, your job may have changed dramatically, while in others your job may have changed little. Yet you probably have changed as a result of going to war, so your approach to your job responsibilities will be different.

Communicate your enthusiasm about coming back. You may not feel so excited to return to work. Your view of the world, including your work, may have changed significantly while you were away. Even so, it's a bad idea to go back to work with a "Take this job and shove it" attitude. Even if you aren't looking forward to your job, the old adage "Fake it 'til you make it" applies. You may realize after you've been back at work for a while that the job still has worthwhile benefits. Give yourself time to acclimate before saying or doing anything you may later regret. Your current employment may be a springboard to your next job; resuming it in a professional manner is important so it won't hinder future job leads or connections.

Thank those who helped out during your absence. Some of your coworkers or colleagues may have pitched in to keep things running while you were gone. Make sure you thank them for their extra effort, and ask them how they've been doing in your absence. Some may have faced difficult situations outside work while you were away, and they may assume you're aware of these circumstances when in fact you aren't. Showing interest in them will foster goodwill and help make the work environment more collaborative and supportive for everybody.

Be clear from the beginning about what you want to tell others. As you make an effort to check in with your coworkers, supervisors, or customers, don't be surprised if many of them want to do the same with you. Although some may be motivated by concern for you, others may simply be curious. Still others may have negative opinions about the war and your involvement in it. Regardless, you should decide before returning to work how you'll respond to questions that others are bound to ask you about the war. Have a game plan in mind about what you'll say. You may want to be clear from the beginning, for example, that you'll answer questions about the general climate, culture, and environment of where you were stationed, but that you won't discuss specific combat missions you were on or duties you performed.

Consider transitioning slowly back to full-time work status. A slow transition to a full-time schedule may be the best option for you and your family. Will your adjustment to work go more smoothly if you use a graduated schedule, working a few hours a day or a few full days a week to start? What kind of flexibility will your employer offer you? If he or she can't change your schedule to let you transition more slowly, can your workload be lightened to allow you time to readjust to the job?

Don't make a quick decision to change jobs. After giving yourself at least six to nine months back on the job, you may discover that it's no longer satisfying, and you may seriously consider leaving. If so, make a list of what you like and dislike about your job, including any benefits you receive such as a 401(k) plan, a retirement plan, or vacation time. If you're married or in a domestic partnership, share this list with your partner and get his or her input. After weighing the pros and cons of your current job carefully, if you decide to leave, you should have a new position waiting for you. Don't quit abruptly without having another job lined up.

Coming Home to No Job

Some people returning home from war unexpectedly find that their employer's company has folded. Or they may come home to discover that their job has been eliminated. Such news can be tremendously unsettling. Job disappointments can intensify emotional challenges you might already be dealing with from your deployment. Stressful life events like a job loss affect how you view your military service to our country. What you tell yourself about difficulties like these can help shape how you think about the sacrifices you made while in the war zone.

Although losing a job can be devastating at the time, it also can be one of the best things to happen because it causes you to reevaluate what you want from work. If you come home to no job, or if you decide to leave the military after your most recent deployment and you're not hard pressed to find new work, it can be helpful to spend time figuring out exactly what you want to do. You can go to a vocational counselor through your local VA hospital or to a job coach in the private sector to help you explore career options. Books and websites can also help you identify your professional interests and skills. Creating and maintaining structure in your life can help you stay focused on finding work. After living in a regimented military environment, it may be hard to buckle down and find a new job. Build a routine into your day as you look for employment. Treat this search as if it's a job and you're the boss.

Serving in a war may affect what career path you choose. Your experience in Iraq or Afghanistan may steer you away from some jobs, including the job you had before you were deployed, and toward others. Make sure that what you choose to pursue is something you can see yourself doing for at least a few years. Your work experience in the military is something you can highlight on your résumé. It can be an example of your dedication, hard work, leadership, and ability to handle stress. Many employers will see these characteristics as positive and useful.

If you don't have the luxury of taking time to look for employment, you may need to find temporary work while you consider your job interests and opportunities. Look for a temporary job that will give you the flexibility to figure out what you really want to do.

CONSIDER SCHOOL

When **John** returned home from Afghanistan he had no idea what he would do. He thought about working full-time but thought it might be a bit overwhelming. While in Afghanistan he became interested in how the media portrayed the war. He decided to take a couple of film classes at San Francisco City College. Three weeks into the school semester, while his instructor was lecturing on the history of film, he kept thinking about his last day in combat, when his good friend was killed. He couldn't concentrate and left class early. He talked about this experience with both his professor and his classmate, Phil, who was also a veteran. His professor was able to be flexible about homework assignments and met with John to go over the material he missed when he left class early. Phil agreed to touch his shoulder during class if he thought John appeared to be preoccupied with thoughts about his war experience. John was relieved to have both his friend and his professor watching out for him.

If you don't have a job to return to and you have the time, interest, and finances, going to school may be a good option for you. But school can be an incredibly odd experience after having served in a war zone. While many work environments don't provide much time for reflection because of busy schedules and numerous responsibilities, most school programs provide an opportunity to daydream and be idle. In the classroom, you're likely to feel very different from your peers, who probably have

RETURNING TO CIVILIAN LIFE ✦ 157

no idea what you experienced. For example, one returning veteran from Iraq who enrolled in a graduate school for psychology remarked on how strange it was to be in a classroom full of students with very different views from hers about the war. She was bothered by how little they actually knew about the sacrifice she and others had made for them. In the long run, talking with her fellow students proved to be a useful endeavor, allowing her to influence the ways in which some peers viewed the military.

Returning to school does have some significant advantages over full-time work. You have more flexibility in choosing when and how to accomplish your assignments. There is structure at school, but not too much structure. Instructors may be willing to negotiate time frames, while bosses at work may not be so flexible. For some returning veterans, not having to deal with the authoritarian environment that exists at many work situations is a blessing. School can also provide time to help sort out what career path to choose and to stimulate interests you didn't think about while deployed. By taking a variety of courses, you can clarify what you want to do. And a college or graduate school degree can lead to new, possibly lucrative or satisfying employment opportunities outside the military.

Here are some suggestions for beginning or returning to school postdeployment:

- Don't take too big a course load. If you have the option, it's probably better to ease into schoolwork and not overwhelm yourself with too many classes.
- Stay focused on class materials and lectures as much as possible, to keep your mind from wandering back to war experiences or memories. Taking notes during class can help you stay focused.
- Get involved in school activities as a way to break down what you perceive as barriers between you and classmates. Even if you have different views about the war or politics,

you can connect with classmates around a shared activity such as a team project, a club, or a sport.

- Accept that there will be some students and instructors who don't like the fact that you were in Iraq or Afghanistan. Realize that you may have to limit your contact with such individuals.

- Take advantage of all school services available to you. Many colleges and universities have school counselors to consult with about career issues. School counseling centers may provide free or low-cost therapy services. If you feel that you need additional academic assistance, tutoring services are probably available as well.

- Consult with veterans' representatives about school and funding. Some schools have representatives who know the difficulties that returning veterans like you may be experiencing. They can help you complete the necessary paperwork to enter or reenter school, and they can provide support for managing the school process. Ask these representatives or the appropriate military office about what school funds you're eligible for as a veteran, such as the GI Bill, and take full advantage of them.

- Consider combining work and school. Although you may not have the financial luxury to go to school full-time, working and going to school can mean the best of both worlds. Through this combined approach, you may be able to get the structure and income you need from work while achieving the freedom and intellectual challenge you desire from school. Be careful, though, not to become too busy with school, work, or both. Sometimes engrossing oneself at school or work is a way to avoid feelings and memories from your military experience. It may work in the short run, but over the long run avoiding feelings and memories may interfere with your adjustment home. If you're too immersed in school or work and becoming a "schoolaholic" or "workaholic," it may be a sign that you need to develop other coping strategies.

Readjusting to the Community

Sarah recently returned home to Tampa, Florida, from Iraq and now lives with her parents. She rarely ventures out into her old neighborhood and has declined many invitations to get together with friends and extended family members. Her parents are worried, but they aren't sure whether to press her to go out or to leave her alone.

War has a way of making returning veterans feel "different." Often veterans describe themselves as outcasts or loners. You may think that civilians can't possibly understand what you have gone through, so your tendency is to withdraw and stay at home. You may feel disconnected from the people living in your neighborhood. Perhaps you don't even want people in your community to know that you served in Iraq or Afghanistan. So the last thing you probably want to do is get involved in your community. But participating in social, political, professional, or volunteer activities in your community will help you feel connected to others, and you'll feel good about making a contribution to society at large. In turn, this involvement will ease your readjustment to civilian life.

As you return to civilian life, you have the opportunity to get involved in your community at many levels. You may not realize it, but your wartime experience has equipped you with unique skills that can be used to strengthen your community and the larger society around you, from your immediate neighborhood to your school district, your state, or even your country. Your military participation in Iraq or Afghanistan has helped to provide Americans with safe and free communities at home. Take advantage of the democratic society you fought so hard for by getting involved. Find the aspect of your community that's meaningful to you and participate in it as much as you can.

Here's a list of community-oriented activities you might participate in.

Veteran organizations. Groups geared specifically toward returning veterans like you can be a good place to socialize. They may offer the most comfortable setting for you to become involved in. Many veterans remark that VA hospitals, vet centers, and veterans groups such as the Veterans of Foreign Wars (VFW) feel like a second home because other veterans who also attend "really understand."

Schools. Whether you have children or not, schools in your community are a place where you can develop relationships, contribute in meaningful ways, and help influence the education of children. There are many school projects you can become involved in, such as organizing fund-raisers, which entails a great deal of contact with others, or tutoring children one-on-one, which requires much less contact with large groups. You can also volunteer at your local school to talk about your experiences during the war. This service can help teach schoolchildren about the sacrifices our men and women in uniform have made. Although giving a talk like this may be emotionally difficult, it can help you feel more connected to the community.

Church, synagogue, temple, or mosque. A place of worship can be an important venue to develop a sense of community and belonging. Not only does a place of worship help you find meaning in your life, but it can also help you build new connections with others, provide you with spiritual guidance, and give you a broader perspective of the world and of what war represents.

Sports leagues. Sports clubs for you or your children provide another structured way to interact with others. They provide a framework for developing new relationships and broadening your connections in the community. At the same time, they can help you or your children stay in shape. You may want to consider coaching or providing additional support to one of your children's teams as well.

Neighborhood activities. Become involved in your neighborhood by organizing block parties, creating watch groups, or cleaning up the local park. Help your neighbors with small projects such as gardening or babysitting as a way to forge better relationships with those around you.

Community projects. In addition to neighborhood involvement, partake in larger-scale community service activities, such as building a playground, visiting the elderly, doing team-in-training or a walkathon for a cause, teaching computer skills to the underserved, or cleaning up the beach. Volunteering your time in these ways can be both rewarding and fun.

Professional organizations. Groups based on a common professional interest can also be a great place to connect with others and can provide structure to the interaction. These organizations may be affiliated with your work or may give you a foot in the door to a new field of employment you're interested in.

Hobbies. Whether it's motorcycles, basketball, coin collecting, cooking, or hang gliding, organizations that are built around a common interest can be enjoyable and may provide you with a structured social outlet.

Internet. While the Internet can be a wonderful tool to help you find resources or connect with others, it can also be a barrier between you and the community you live in. Don't spend all your time online! Monitor how much time you spend on the Internet. If you're online more than two hours each day, and this time isn't specifically related to school, work, or a project, consider scaling back to one to two hours each day. In place of your Web surfing time, get out and meet new people or reconnect with old friends in your community.

Text continued on page 164.

WHAT EMPLOYERS SHOULD KNOW OR DO TO HELP IRAQ AND AFGHANISTAN VETERANS RETURN TO WORK

Returning veterans who reenter work at your job site are struggling with many emotions and reactions related to their deployment, including anxiety and stress. As their employer, you can play a major role in making their transition home smoother by reviewing the suggestions that follow. How you welcome these men and women back can make a profound difference in their emotional state. If you demonstrate an understanding of the stress they feel about their overseas experience and the challenge of returning home, they'll be likely to see you as an ally who really cares about them. In return, they'll be more likely to become motivated to work hard for you and to be loyal to your organization. Here are tips for you to take into account when these employees return to work.

Top 6 Tips for Employers

1. Meet with the returning employee before the first day back at the job. This will help clarify expectations and establish his or her successful return to your organization's work environment. If possible, provide him or her with written information about how job responsibilities have changed. This will give him or her time to digest the new expectations you have. Some of the issues to address in writing are:

- The work environment—what's different and what's the same? Provide information and a timeline about what has changed at the workplace.
- The specific job the worker does—what's different and what's the same? Provide specific information about how the worker's job is different and specific instructions to aid him or her in adapting to the new environment.
- The performance expectations—what are the job expectations for the first few weeks? Outline these as specifically as possible so the returning employee has specific goals to work toward. To ease the adjustment during this initial period, be flexible and come up with an individualized plan for each returning veteran who works for you. This doesn't mean "any-

thing goes." Develop realistic expectations that both you and the returning employee can agree to. It doesn't do employees any good if you pretend they're doing a job successfully when they aren't. It can be more damaging to their self-esteem and work ethic in the long run if you put off responding to any difficulties they may be having.

2. Besides holding this meeting and providing written information about work issues, ask the returning employee specific work readjustment questions such as these:

- What schedule works best? What kind of schedule does this employee think he or she can realistically adhere to, taking into account family obligations and postwar reactions? Should he or she begin full-time, or is there the option to start part-time and gradually move to full-time? Can he or she take time off for medical appointments and family meetings to help with stateside adjustment?

- How is he or she doing emotionally? While this may not be your area of expertise, communicating your support for the emotional well-being of the employee will go a long way toward helping him or her feel positive about returning to the workplace.

- How is he or she doing financially? Not only is the war-zone experience difficult emotionally for returning veterans, but many return to financial problems that they wouldn't have had if they hadn't been deployed. For some, the time away meant surviving on their military pay. Others may have missed a raise or promotion. Still others may have lost retirement benefits or been short-changed on overtime pay that they used to depend on to make ends meet. These financial changes may make them feel as though they're being punished instead of rewarded for serving their country. Consider loans, advance pay, or other programs you can offer returning employees to help with their financial difficulties. Can you advocate on their behalf, for instance, to recover lost retirement benefits or lost promotions?

(Text continued on pages 164–65.)

• Is he or she interested in having a welcome-home party? Some veterans may want one, while others may tend to shy away from such events. Veterans may have intense ambivalence about any kind of acknowledgment that celebrates their return. The reasons for this can vary. Some veterans may object to any sort of welcome-home party because they feel it compares their sacrifice to that of other service personnel who came back injured or didn't come back at all. The tone in which veterans discuss their war-zone experience (or the fact that they don't) may also help you determine whether or not to hold such an event. *Regardless of whether you hold one, make sure you express sincere appreciation on behalf of your organization for their service to the country.*

3. Provide the returning employee with the opportunity to tell his or her story, if appropriate. Your role is not to be a therapist for your employees. But for some returning veterans, allowing them to talk in bits and pieces about their war experience can be helpful. Whether you provide this opportunity will depend on your relationship with them and the nature or culture of your workplace.

4. Provide the returning employee with more than one welcome-home meeting or event. One of the big complaints returning veterans have is that though they may be enthusiastically welcomed

Local politics. You can fight for a local political issue that you find important by sitting on an advisory panel or council or speaking at community lectures, and it can be an empowering experience. Remember, it's not whether you win but whether you play the game that counts.

National politics. Working for a political candidate or a party that you feel best represents your beliefs is another way of exercising your power as a citizen. Writing letters to your state or national senator or congressperson to express your political views, can be particularly effective when you highlight your veteran status.

home by family, friends, and the larger community on their homecoming, they and their military service are quickly forgotten. The feeling of being abandoned is a significant problem for returning veterans as they attempt to make sense of what they went through at war. It can help a great deal if you can provide additional meetings throughout the year to see how they're adjusting, or at least remind them that you appreciate the sacrifices they made.

5. Assume success. Begin with the expectation that the returning employee is quite capable of performing his or her job. That he or she survived the war and completed his or her tour shows a great deal of courage and tenacity. Don't assume that everyone who serves in war returns emotionally damaged. The fact is, after the initial period of adjustment, the majority of Iraq and Afghanistan veterans will be as capable and emotionally stable as they were when they left.

6. Use employee assistance programs, human resources, and veterans' services as appropriate. Employee assistance programs and Veterans Administration services, both at outpatient hospitals and vet centers, can help with employees' reentry into the workforce. Don't hesitate to contact these service providers for ideas about what you can do to help veterans make a successful reentry into your workplace and become a valued employee again.

Remember, you don't have to like everybody you deal with to participate in activities with them. You won't get along with all people in every walk of life; but the opposite is also true. You may find friendships in all sorts of places that you wouldn't have expected. The crucial goal is to interact with people in your community. The more you socialize, the better you'll become at combating the negative aspects of your war experience. Getting involved in your community is a powerful way to fight back, and to keep your war experience from having a negative impact on how you see yourself and the world.

"Dumb" Questions Civilians Ask and How to Respond to Them

You will encounter people who discover that you served in Iraq or Afghanistan and will ask you questions that show their ignorance about war or the armed services. While some of these people may ask questions to try to upset you, most are truly oblivious to the impact their questions have on you. Think of a bad accident on the highway. Traffic slows down mostly because other drivers have a morbid curiosity about what happened. This type of reaction is also why many nonmilitary people ask questions about your war experience.

Among the questions and comments that may be thrown at you at any time, by anyone, are these:

How was it?

Did you kill anyone?

Are you like those "crazy" Vietnam vets?

Did you read about . . . that happened over there?

What do you think about Abu Ghraib?

Why aren't you still in Iraq (or Afghanistan)?

How did you get out of going to Iraq (or Afghanistan)?

How come you "only" did one tour?

It's a good thing you didn't have to see any combat (said to a female veteran who saw combat).

Here are some of the ways you can respond to these questions and comments:

- Practice or rehearse how to respond so you'll be prepared when these questions are raised. You can practice with your partner or a friend, or you can write out your responses on index cards. The more you practice, the better you'll be able to respond in a calm, cool, collected manner.

- Use your sense of humor to deescalate potential tension or discomfort. Humor can often break the seriousness of these awkward moments and move the conversation on to a more comfortable topic. For example, a veteran learned to respond to people who asked him how it was to serve overseas by saying, "Well, if you really want to know about what it was like there, I hear the military is still looking for a few good men and women . . . "
- Ignore the question or respond to it by deflecting or redirecting the conversation onto another topic. For example, you can simply say, "I'd rather not talk about that right now. How have things been for you over the past few months?" Or "It was a challenging experience that I'm adjusting to. I'd rather focus on what's going on here now that I'm home." Or "Let's talk about something else. I don't want to talk about that now."
- Educate the people who ask these questions. You may actually find that some truly appreciate what you have to tell them. For example, you might say, "The war situation is a lot more complicated than it appears. I'd like to tell you more about my real experience there, if you're really interested and have the time," or "I have strong opinions about the war and would be glad to share them with you if you're willing to listen." Depending on how the person responds, you can choose how to proceed.

Sometimes children who are struggling to understand war and death will ask these kinds of challenging questions. In your answers, try to use simple, clear language to describe the challenges of war without providing too much detail.

Text continued on page 170.

SERVICE-CONNECTED DISABILITY COMPENSATION

If you believe you incurred medical or psychological injuries, or both, during your military service, you may want to apply for a service-connected disability compensation rating. The U.S. Government compensates its military service veterans for in-service emotional and physical disabilities. The advantage of obtaining the rating is that it may entitle you to receive a monthly compensation check for an extended time (sometimes for your lifetime) and to get higher-priority care at VA facilities (which may mean free or low-cost health care). The amount of money the Veterans Administration provides you will vary, depending on the percentage of service-connected disability it determines you've suffered.

APPLYING FOR A SERVICE-CONNECTED DISABILITY COMPENSATION RATING

If you decide to apply for a disability compensation rating, file a claim with the Department of Veterans Affairs Veterans Benefits Administration (VBA). Provide the VBA with your discharge papers (your DD214) and information about your injuries, including doctors' statements and a "stressor statement" documenting how you became injured during your military service. Instructions for filling out a service-connection claim application can be found by going to www.seamlesstransition.va.gov/seamlesstransition/benefits.asp, then clicking on the Compensation and Benefits icon. Since filing an application is complicated, the information on this website can be extremely helpful.

Writing a stressor statement can be especially challenging because you will be writing about when you were injured, which may bring up the most upsetting or traumatic part of your military experience. Understandably, this process can trigger all sorts of uncomfortable memories and feelings. So you may want to write your stressor statement with your partner, a family member, a close friend, or another veteran who has gone through the process. You can also enlist the help of a professional who assists veterans in filing their claims. These professionals, called Veteran Benefits

Representatives or Veteran Service Officers (see pages 211 and 227 in the "Resources" section), can help you free of charge. Getting help from someone may ease the stress of writing this important statement.

After you submit your paperwork, the VBA will determine whether your claim should be reviewed by medical specialists in the area of your disability. If those specialists agree with your claim, you'll be scheduled for a Compensation and Pension rating examination. Depending on your claim, you may be examined by more than one person. These examinations typically include an evaluation of your level of functioning in the areas of work, school, and social functioning. They may include an evaluation of any psychological or medical problems you're having that relate to your service time. These evaluations, along with your medical chart, stressor statement, and any additional outside medical reports you have, will be sent to a claims processing rating board composed of a physician and rating specialists, who will determine your level of disability.

LET GO OF THE OUTCOME

The VBA will decide how disabled they believe you are as a result of the injury or injuries you received in the military. Their decision can be appealed, but if you wish to file an appeal, be sure to submit a notice of disagreement within one year of the date of the board's decision. When the VBA makes their ruling, they will send you a letter. This decision can be emotionally upsetting. You may feel your award is too small, that the government doesn't understand the extent of your injuries and once again has let you down. Or, if you receive a large award, you may find yourself happy at first but then wonder what it means that the government sees you as significantly "disabled." It's easy to become obsessed by this whole process— and enraged if you don't get what you think you deserve. You may need to use some of the coping strategies in this book to handle this difficult process. Try not to place too much emphasis on the outcome of your service-connection claim. Remember, no amount of money can ever repay you for the sacrifice you've made for your country.

TIPS FOR PARTNERS, FAMILY MEMBERS, AND FRIENDS

As a family member, you can use some of the following strategies to help your veteran readjust to work, school, and the community.

Allow your veteran to acclimate at his or her own pace. You may become impatient with the pace of your veteran's transition, but try to stay calm. Remember that if you become reactive, you probably won't help the situation but instead will add to your loved one's stress. You too may benefit from reading this chapter and the coping chapters in this book.

Help provide structure for your veteran. Aid him or her in establishing a daily schedule to follow. For example, set up routines for going to bed, getting up, exercising, and eating. This will help him or her focus, especially if he or she has no external structure such as a job or school.

Attend social functions with your veteran. Returning service men and women may be reluctant to participate in social activities, so smaller gatherings or less-stressful social functions are a good place to begin. A returning veteran will often be more irritable and feel unsafe in large social functions. You can help increase your veteran's feelings of comfort and safety by discussing the event in some detail before going there and making sure he or she can talk with you about leaving early if things get overwhelming. Talk with your veteran about what might be difficult for him or her if he or she attends the event. During the social function, it may be helpful to sit where your veteran can see the door exits or have his or her back against a wall. Choose events that have the potential for fun. Afterward, devote some time to discussing how the event went. Social events may become somewhat easier as the veteran attends more of them, or the process may ebb and flow depending on how your veteran responds to war reminders he or she may encounter.

Use your own family or community connections. Help your veteran find work or participate in the community by using your own family resources and community connections.

Get involved politically. You may feel helpless if your veteran is not accepting your support or is having a hard time following through with your suggestions. If so, consider helping him or her by directing your energy toward larger issues of veterans' rights or other organizations that help veterans, while continuing to provide support to your own veteran.

Take care of yourself. Make sure you're focusing on your own needs as well as those of your veteran. For instance, go out and socialize with your friends, even if your returning veteran isn't ready for that. In some cases, it can take a long time before a veteran will be interested in socializing. Instead of completely cutting yourself off from family and friends to be with him or her, make sure you spend some time maintaining your relationships with others. These connections will help you maintain your energy and keep your spirits up.

After a reasonable period of time (up to four months), if you don't think your veteran is adjusting back to work, school, or the community, ask to talk with him or her about your concerns. If you think his or her difficulties may be serious, encourage him or her to seek professional help.

The recommendations in the box on page 162 can be useful for your veteran's civilian employer, and you may want to share this with him or her.

7

Restoring Family Roles and Relationships

Fighting in a war can fracture your connection with the world, making you feel very alone. After someone experiences war, connecting with others becomes much more difficult. Because war often involves loss or threat of loss, you might worry that others won't be there for you when you need them, even now that you're home. And after being deployed for some time, family roles may have shifted. But relationships, especially with family members, can be *the* healing antidote to the experiences of war. This chapter covers how to adjust to role changes that have occurred in your family since you've been away and how to have conversations with adult family members about your war experiences.

It will also provide tips on how to restore and improve your relationship with your partner and how to reconnect with and discipline your children. And it will give suggestions to your parents about how they can help you transition home.

Feeling a "Part" after Being Apart

Erin, a Navy medic who served in Afghanistan, feels different than she did before she served. She's surprised to discover that she doesn't know how to fit back in with the family she once felt so close to. She feels out of place and useless, even in her own home.

While you were away, family members probably took on new household roles that were yours before you left. Your family had to adapt to your not being there, so they developed new strategies to function. These roles could be as simple as who cuts the grass, takes out the garbage, washes the dishes, drives the kids to school, or pays the bills.

Such roles also include providing emotional support to members of the family while you were gone. Emotional support roles may have been taken on by extended family or friends. When you return home, you may feel out of place or jealous that your kids have gotten into the habit of going to your partner or a relative for help or advice instead of coming to you. You may feel useless and unneeded as you see how competently your family has functioned without you.

Family members may have difficulty giving up their new roles. They might try to protect you by sparing you from household chores. Although you're probably thankful that your family has been able to care for themselves and reach out to others for help, how do you find your place back into the family? The way you communicate can affect how quickly you get back on track with your loved ones. It's important to have an honest discussion with your family about role changes. Tell them how you want to make a contribution to the family, and negotiate taking back certain responsibilities or even picking up new ones.

Tips for Reuniting with Your Family

Go slow! Spend time getting to know each member of the family all over again. Try not to be judgmental when you're learning what's new about your family. It may be a challenge to do this, but it will help you understand your family and the choices they've made.

Be curious about your family. Get to know how your family functioned without you. In what ways did they change, and why? How can you appreciate what they went through?

Learn the new routine. Work with your partner to assess what aspects of the "new routine" you two want to keep and what parts you want to change.

Discover new family strengths. Help support the changes your family has made while you were away that they feel good about, and compliment them on these newly discovered family strengths even though this may not be easy to do.

Don't leave disagreements unresolved. You and your partner may not agree about whether some of the changes that have occurred are beneficial. But work toward an understanding of the issues; don't avoid talking about them. If you can't find a way to compromise or successfully negotiate your differences, you may want to seek the help of a professional, such as a therapist or a member of the clergy, to help you through these difficulties.

Talking about Your War Experiences with Supportive Adults

Hector, a returning veteran from Iraq, feels that he has to keep secrets from his wife about what he did while he was deployed. He fears that if he told her the truth, she would see him as violent, crazy, or even evil.

Many people's reaction to a traumatic experience like war is to put up an emotional wall and not tell anybody about what they saw or did during that time.

You may be experiencing this same reaction. You can't stop thinking about your war experiences, yet you don't dare tell those close to you about them. During war, you were faced with deadly situations that you never could have imagined. You made split-second, life-or-death decisions. You were exposed to electrifying fear you never felt before. You witnessed and participated in the unthinkable. You wonder how anybody who wasn't there could possibly comprehend what you've been through.

Let's look more deeply at why you may be hesitant to talk about your war experiences with adult loved ones such as your spouse, parents, or close friends. Do some of the following reasons ring true for you?

- You fear that you'll infect loved ones, as if what you saw, did, or felt while at war were contagious.
- You fear that they'd no longer love you if they knew what you did there.
- You fear that once you begin talking, you'll lose control, start crying, and be unable to stop your tears.
- You worry about feeling embarrassed or humiliated if you open up.
- You're concerned that you'll appear weak and needy if you share, which goes against your military training and perhaps your upbringing.
- You worry that loved ones will respond with shock, disbelief, silence, anger, or disgust.
- You don't want to burden your family, since you already feel guilty for having been away for so long.
- You fear you'll open up an emotional wound that will hurt both you and your family.

What other concerns do you have about talking to loved ones regarding your war experiences?

If you are having worries like these, you're not alone. Such thoughts and fears make a lot of sense. The mixed feelings, strong reactions, and chaotic events that come with a war experience are complicated and scary. To talk about them with others, even if they're loved ones, is a risky venture into unfamiliar territory.

PITFALLS OF BLACK-OR-WHITE THINKING

After returning from war, people often perceive the world in a more polarized way. Things appear either black or white, good or bad, all or nothing, successes or failures. This black-or-white thinking was natural during combat, when you had no room for error. You couldn't afford any middle ground. Any mistake you made could get you or someone you knew killed. You were the warrior and your opponents were the enemy. Although this black-or-white mentality was useful during war, it's not helpful when applied to how you think about sharing war experiences with loved ones. Why? Because...

- You may feel that you have to tell *everything* you did while you were at war or *nothing* at all. If you're thinking in these terms, it seems logical that you would choose not to share anything, because the risk of sharing everything is overwhelming.

- You may think that the *only* people who will understand what you went through are other veterans. *Nobody* else could ever possibly understand. So why would you even bother to try to share?

BENEFITS OF SHARING

Couples therapist and researcher Dr. John Gottman emphasizes that successful relationships are those in which the partners choose to turn toward each other rather than away. Based on numerous observations of husbands and wives, he has found that couples are less likely to divorce when each partner consistently chooses to respond to the other's invitations for connection, support, and affection by engaging—not by turning away, withdrawing, or withholding.

Keeping Dr. Gottman's findings in mind, consider some possible benefits of talking about your war experiences with adult loved ones—even if you don't share everything—instead of shutting them out. Here are some potential advantages of talking about your wartime experiences:

- You can connect more deeply with loved ones.
- It helps loved ones better understand what you went through and why you now behave and react in certain ways, such as becoming irritable quickly or having trouble sleeping.
- In turn, your loved ones can support you better because they understand more fully what you went through and how it affects you today.
- The shackles of guilt, shame, and secrecy you may feel about war can be loosened when you begin to share.
- When you open up with loved ones, they may feel more comfortable sharing with you the feelings or personal struggles that they experienced during your deployment or at other difficult times in their lives.

How to Talk with Supportive Adults

When individuals who have served in a war zone share their experiences with supportive adults, it creates a win-win situation. The returning veteran feels heard and cared for, while his or her loved ones feel needed and better prepared to help. So once you feel relatively stable and adjusted after your return home, you'll benefit by gradually sharing some information about your war experiences with loved ones. Here are specific suggestions for facilitating such conversations.

SET THE STAGE FOR SHARING

Before you begin talking about your war experiences, ask loved ones what it was like for them while you were away. Show genuine caring and interest about what their lives have been like without you. Like you, they experienced changes and hardship during your deployment. Not only did they have to modify their way of operating as a family, they also worried about your safety, whereabouts, and whether you'd come back alive. As you faced the unpredictable threats of war, they confronted the uncertainty of your return. By trying to understand what their world was like while you were deployed, you make an emotional connection with them that strengthens your bond. Even though you may believe that you kept up with family happenings via e-mail, letters, or occasional phone calls, your loved ones may have shielded you from some of the difficult issues they had to face. You'll need time to consider and respond to what they tell you, so you may want to talk about their experiences for a while before you're ready to share your own war journey.

Selectively choose those adults with whom to share. You'll want to choose people you know you can trust and who are most likely to understand what you have to say. You may want to start with people you've turned to in the past for help or support because they could be counted on to respond in helpful, understanding ways. Evaluate how safe and secure you feel in your relationship with those individuals. If the relationship doesn't feel safe, ask yourself "Is this because of my war experience?" If the answer is "yes," then proceed—but slowly. If your relationship feels unsafe because of other issues that existed before your deployment or arose while you were away, work on addressing those issues *first,* and then move on to talking about your war experiences.

Choose times to talk to loved ones when they're not distracted or pressed for time. Once you've selected supportive adults to talk to, ask them in advance to set aside a mutually agreed-on time to discuss something important to you related to your war experiences. Pick a specific day and time that's convenient for them and you, when they will be mentally and emotionally available. You don't want them to be busy or preoccupied when you have this conversation. Respecting their time and schedules will pay off because they'll be more likely to respond supportively. You may want to reserve the same day and time each week or each month to talk about your war experiences. If you have children, it's best to arrange for a babysitter to watch them, minimizing the possibility of their interrupting or distracting you.

Tell loved ones before beginning how you'd like for them to respond. This is new territory for both you and your loved ones. Telling them how you'd like them to react while you are talking about your war experiences gives them guidelines for being supportive. The more you can explain what you need from them, the more likely you are to receive it. For instance, you may tell them you only want them to listen to you talk without interrupting you. You may want to say this is very hard for you to do, so you need them to show their support and understanding by not asking too many questions or showing reactions of shock or disbelief. You may want to warn them that you could become emotional while talking, but you need them to stick by you. If you're not sure how you would like them to respond, tell them that during the conversation you might need to pause and talk some more about how they can be supportive listeners.

Move away from black-or-white thinking. Don't feel that you need to share everything about your war experiences in one sitting. Be flexible. You don't have to keep everything inside, nor do you have to tell every single detail. You can share in gradual stages over time, perhaps beginning chronologically. For example, you can describe what it was like leading up to deployment and what your expectations were about the war. Then you can tell what it was like when you landed in the war zone, and what your first reactions were. And remember, you don't need to talk only about the bad times of war. You can also share the good, funny, surprising, or interesting times.

Allow for a cool-down time. To ease the transition from talking about your war experience back to day-to-day living, you may want to schedule a cool-down time that will help deescalate the intensity of the conversation about your war experiences so you can more smoothly resume your daily routines. This is not a time to discuss current problems. Instead, engage in fun, lighthearted conversation or activities to help you shift back to the present.

CONSIDER HOW AND WHAT TO SHARE

Various ways of sharing may be less threatening to you and your loved ones, especially at first:

- Share things related to your war experience, such as photographs, war memorabilia, or a journal you kept while deployed, as a springboard for conversation. Choose memorabilia carefully since it may trigger powerful and uncomfortable memories.
- Talk about reactions you're having that are tied to your war experiences. For instance, explain what the experience of having nightmares about war is like. Discuss your fatigue and lack of sleep. Describe how you feel when you see a truck that reminds you of the enemy or hear war-related news. Explain what it feels like when you're easily startled by noises. Describe how hard it is to go back to your job, coming off your war experience.
- Discuss how you're trying to cope with your war experiences. Share survival strategies that you're finding useful and ways that your loved ones can help support you. Share handouts or information you've received from the military or Department of Veterans Affairs about what you're going through so they can better understand.
- Describe a few people who were deployed with you, what they were like, and what you learned from them.
- Talk about how your view of life and the future has changed since being at war.

TIPS FOR ADULT FAMILY MEMBERS: HOW TO RESPOND WHEN YOUR VETERAN TALKS ABOUT WAR

When a veteran chooses to talk about war experiences, loved ones can help the conversation go more smoothly by what they say and do in response. Here are some tips:

- Realize how difficult it is for him or her to open up about war experiences. Make it clear that you recognize how hard it is for him or her to share these experiences with you and how much you appreciate it.
- Show appreciation for your veteran's service to the country. Tell him or her how proud you are and express gratitude for his or her patriotism. Thank your veteran for showing courage and valor not only at war but also at home as he or she readjusts to life with you and your family.
- Reassure your veteran that he or she is safe at home with you. Stress that you want him or her to feel secure and loved and that you're there for him or her unconditionally.
- Validate the hardship your veteran faced at war by focusing on the feelings he or she expresses about war experiences. If he or she has described what it was like to lose a buddy at war, for example, you might respond by saying: "It must have been really hard for you to lose somebody who was by your side in war."
- Be a witness to what he or she has gone through during war, but don't judge. Try to understand your veteran's war journey by paying close attention. Withhold your own opinions or reactions. Envision what he or she has gone through. Empathize, don't evaluate.
- If you've experienced trauma in your own life, you may be able to share parts of it, showing that you can relate to your veteran's traumatic war experiences. By bringing up your own history, though, you may become overwhelmed or extra emotional. Be honest about this and discuss with your veteran how much detail you'll be able to handle.

- Recount a particular event that happened during your deployment or an aspect of your war service that affected you strongly. Tell how you reacted and how it impacts you today.
- Share what it was like to be immersed in a different culture and environment while at war.

Improving Intimate Relationships

Daleesha and Baron were having the same argument they'd had last week about bedtime routines for their children, which had changed during Daleesha's time in Iraq. Instead of talking about how she felt excluded because she wasn't part of putting the kids to bed, Daleesha withdrew from the family, sitting in her room and watching TV. When she could finally discuss her feelings about this situation, Baron acknowledged his contribution to the problem, and they both felt understood. The couple could then have a productive conversation about developing a new bedtime ritual that included both of them, instead of blaming each other and leaving the issue unresolved.

After returning from war, it's important to strengthen the intimacy between you and your partner. All couples have disagreements, but after an extended separation during deployment, the two of you can expect an increase in tension and conflict. The way you express your differences and show that you care for each other will help determine how satisfied you both are in the relationship, how well you adjust back home after your deployment, and how well you reconnect with one another.

STOP THE "DANCE" AND TRY SOMETHING NEW

The experience of war and deployment can invite you and your partner to do all sorts of unproductive "dances." A dance is an interaction or pattern that develops between two people that is usually repetitive and, many times, problematic. It can be so familiar to you that you can watch yourself interact with your partner as if you're on autopilot. You know that what you and your partner are doing isn't good for the relationship but feel almost helpless to stop it.

The first step in breaking this pattern is to team up with your partner. You might say, "We do this dance that is really unhelpful. Let's figure out a way that you and I can team up against this pattern." By seeing the pattern as external to your relationship, you're more able to recognize that your partner is not the obstacle or the enemy. Then you'll be better able to work through the issue at hand. Your reactions to war may actually increase your need to engage in unhelpful, repetitive behaviors because you fear the unknown. Therefore, breaking out of the hypnotic repetitive dance with your partner may be harder than it was before you were deployed. However, the simple but profound idea of taking a risk to try something new in the way you interact, even in a small way, can change the quality of your relationship.

ACKNOWLEDGE YOUR CONTRIBUTION TO PROBLEMS, AND SEE YOUR PARTNER AS HURTING RATHER THAN AS TRYING TO HURT YOU

Although you're used to being on the offensive from your time at war, verbally attacking your partner in your relationship is a strike against the relationship. Instead, honestly acknowledging what you may have done to contribute to the difficulties at hand can lead to a relationship home run. After you fess up, your partner is more likely to feel interested in helping you. Also, if you're able to see your partner not as "bad" but as in pain, you're more likely to understand his or her perspective and be able to talk about the root of the problem. This will boost intimacy and reduce the likelihood of verbal attacks that cause cumulative distress on the relationship. A noncombative approach often leads to a less defensive stance in your partner and to a more productive conversation and healthy relationship.

GET TO KNOW YOUR PARTNER'S WORLD

After returning from war, take time to understand your partner's perspective, world, and dreams. The couples therapist and researcher Dr. John Gottman has written about the significance of knowing your partner's hopes and intentions, and family therapist Dr. Ron Taffel has written about this same issue in relation to parents knowing the world of their children. Perhaps the stress you face at work or the anxiety you confront when you recall memories of war are interfering with your ability to be close with your partner. Asking questions about your partner's world is critical to fostering a stronger connection. Don't wait for your partner to come to you! To build intimacy, ask questions such as:

- What do you like most/least about your work, school, or taking care of the children?
- What movies/books have you most enjoyed?
- What are your dreams for the future?
- Who are your two closest friends?
- What do you want most in our relationship?

The more you know about your partner, the easier it will be to connect with him or her, and the more your partner will want to connect with you.

USE TOUCH AS A WAY TO RECONNECT

For couples where absence has created a tremendous distance, even the touch of your partner's hand can be comforting. Discussing with her or him what you miss about that touch is a good way to start a dialogue about the impact of your separation. Back, foot, or neck rubs can also help communicate how important your partner is to you. For some couples, their sexual relationship is a key component of connection. Men sometimes feel that it's the *only* way they can connect with their spouse. Sex with the person you love can help soothe the loneliness and emptiness you may feel as a result of your war experience. If you haven't engaged in sexual relations for a long time, it may be important to go slowly and talk about what obstacles may be getting in the way of connecting sexually and how to overcome them.

GIVE YOUR PARTNER MORE COMPLIMENTS

Compliments can improve closeness and reduce the intensity of arguments. At first your partner may not believe you, or you may feel awkward paying compliments. But sincere compliments show affection, attention, and caring, so they can help your partner see you in a more positive light. Try experimenting with this strategy and see if it strengthens your relationship.

PAY ATTENTION TO WHAT IS WORKING IN THE RELATIONSHIP AND GIVE THESE POSITIVE ASPECTS AIRTIME

Couples who are in distress after one or both have been deployed tend to focus exclusively on what's *not* working, which can lead you to look for what's wrong instead of what's right in the relationship. This doesn't mean you should ignore problems. Far from it. It's just that when most of what you discuss with your partner is about what's wrong, your problems gain power over your life. If you spend some time looking at what *is* working in the relationship, it will strengthen your mutual bond, even though you might find it easier to tell your partner what he or she is doing wrong. For example, instead of telling your partner, "You never spend time with the kids," a better way to influence her or him is to say, "I really like it when you spend time with the kids." This approach will also help you more successfully tackle other unresolved issues in the relationship.

ASSUME THAT WHEN YOUR PARTNER IS UPSET, HE OR SHE IS REALLY INTERESTED IN CONNECTING WITH YOU, NOT HURTING YOU

Many times in relationships, the best solution is not to *fix* the problem but to spend time *listening* to your partner. If you were exposed to combat, you may find yourself trying to immediately solve the problem instead of listening to your partner's distress. He or she may not even need you to find a solution but needs you to listen to how distressed he or she is over a particular issue. Supportive comments may help soothe your partner tremendously. Listening shows your partner that you care enough to hear about his or her worries.

SEE CONFLICTS AS OPPORTUNITIES FOR CONNECTION

Understanding why your partner finds an issue to be so highly charged will help you better understand his or her emotional world. If you're genuinely curious about your partner's world, you can create an intense connection that will improve intimacy in your relationship. This is a powerful weapon for combating war trauma while also bringing you closer together.

RECOGNIZE THAT THERE IS NO "PERFECT" PARTNER OR "PERFECT" RELATIONSHIP

We have images in our minds of what the perfect relationship should look like. We all know the *Leave It to Beaver* type family, in which couples easily solve their problems, kids behave themselves, and life goes on without difficulties. These images can create an unrealistic view of relationships and cause people to develop unreasonable expectations. For some, when they realize that their partner doesn't fit the criteria for "perfect," they end the relationship. Those in successful relationships, by contrast, work hard to accept that "imperfect" is okay.

USE "I" STATEMENTS

Focus on your partner's behavior, not character, and take responsibility for your own feelings. The use of "I" statements during a disagreement can keep the conversation from getting out of control. Remember meeting Daleesha and Baron earlier in this chapter? Daleesha was able to tell Baron, "I feel hurt that I am not getting to put the kids to bed at night." Baron interpreted this "I" statement positively. If Daleesha had started the conversation off by saying, "You never think about me and what I need," Baron would probably have reacted defensively. The problem with "I" statements is that people tend not to use them when needed and instead use them when they aren't needed. So you really need to practice using them in situations that are mildly hard to handle so you'll have them as part of your repertoire when a really difficult situation comes along. This strategy will help you listen more and react less. An important rule is to try to stay focused on the issue and not attack your partner's character. Avoid all-or-nothing thinking when it comes to seeing your partner's behaviors. Phrases like "You always . . ." or "you never . . ." can spark a defensive response.

BE WILLING TO APOLOGIZE

Win the relationship, not the fight. Remember to keep what's really important in perspective. Many things that couples find themselves in disagreement over are really not that significant. Unfortunately, at the time, an argument can feel like a life-or-death struggle. This isn't surprising, since returning veterans can have the same physiological response during an argument that they had during combat. A key ingredient for keeping things in perspective is your willingness to apologize when you've upset your partner. This apology can establish a sense of goodwill between the two of you.

WHEN TALKING ABOUT A PROBLEM, STAY FOCUSED

Couples tend to "problem-hop." They move from one unresolved issue to the next. The problems then accumulate, and nothing gets resolved. After returning from war, you have a lot to deal with. It's easy to jump from one pending problem to the next as you try to catch up on everything that happened while you were away.

When talking about a problem, try to focus on a single topic by:

- Agreeing to be respectful, to listen, and to not interrupt.
- Clearly defining the problem and then trying to brainstorm solutions with your partner. Write down all your potential solutions on a piece of paper, and then evaluate the merits of each solution.
- Remembering that problems aren't easily resolved; many are never resolved. Set a maximum length of time for discussing the problem. This time period will vary. The key point is to both agree and abide by the rules you've created.

FIGURE OUT WHAT PROBLEMS ARE SOLVABLE, AND ACCEPT WHAT PROBLEMS ARE NOT

Marital researchers Dr. Robert Levinson and Dr. John Gottman have conducted studies in which couples discuss relationship problems at five-year intervals. One of the most interesting findings from these studies is something that many therapists and couples already know: The majority of disagreements you have with your partner will be lifelong. It's really a matter of living with your partner's different perspectives. This doesn't mean you should live with affairs or allow your partner to abuse you. But it does mean that working hard to get your partner to manage finances exactly the way you want is a waste of time. Working with your partner to figure out strategies for each of you to deal with your differences is a better way to use your energy. How do you know which problems are solvable and which ones you will need to live with? It depends on the couple and how you and your partner feel about a particular issue. If you keep on fighting about the same issue over and over again, you and your partner need to come up with a different problem-solving strategy, because your attempts to influence your partner are backfiring.

TAKE TIME-OUTS WHEN THINGS FEEL OUT OF CONTROL

Moments of intensity between you and your partner can provide a powerful window into what's going on in your emotional lives. On the other hand, you want to make sure that you don't say or do anything in the relationship that you might regret. If you or your partner is worried about losing it, take a time-out. A key ingredient of effective time-outs is to avoid using your away time to think up justifications for your position but instead to clear your head and calm down. Also, make sure your partner knows you're taking a time out and when you will return.

For example, when Daleesha and Baron got into a heated discussion about Daleesha's work, Baron would get upset and take a time-out. Unfortunately, he neglected to tell Daleesha when he'd be back. This increased her feelings of abandonment and her sense that she couldn't count on him. When he did return, she'd berate him about a different issue, which would increase his need to withdraw. By giving Daleesha a time when he'd return and be willing to talk more about the issue, Baron changed the way they used time-outs. It provided them both with a new way to interact and helped them negotiate their concerns more successfully.

LAUGH AND HAVE FUN

Laughing with your partner about external stressors can strengthen your connection. You can introduce humor into your disagreements by making fun of your own behavior. Humor may help to relax both you and your partner and lead to better resolution of disagreements. Schedule time with your partner to engage in mutually pleasurable activities. In our busy lives, sometimes we need to schedule fun activities to make sure they happen. These pleasurable times can help you remember why you're with your partner, especially when you're also dealing with issues that are not so fun.

Reconnecting with Children

Whether you're a parent, a close aunt or uncle, or an older sibling, you may have found that it's been hard to reconnect with children with whom you were close prior to deployment. You may have dreamt of joyful reunions only to return to a shy and withdrawn 9-year-old or an angry and willful adolescent. The infant that you cuddled in your arms before deployment may now be running through the house, terrorizing the cat and tearing at your Sunday paper. Although you may have had some video contact with your family and noticed some of the changes in your children, it still does not capture what the experience is like "live and in color." These changes can be positively jolting! It's understandable that you might wish for a time machine that would allow you to transform your pierced and makeup-wearing teenager back into "Daddy's little girl." This desire, however, to have everything just as it was when you left, can make reconnecting, particularly with children, more difficult. What can you do to connect the child of your memories with the one who stands (or slouches) before you today? Here are a few suggestions for bridging the gap and getting reacquainted:

❑ Enlist the help of your partner or other family members. Ask them to tell you about the child's experiences, good and bad, while you were away. This should include photographs and descriptions of outings and activities, celebrations, successes and failures, school experiences, relationships with friends and family, and ways in which the child has changed while you were away.

❑ Ask your child to show you what you missed. This can include things such as photographs, artwork, or mementos, new toys or clothing, or favorite music or books.

❑ Ask your child simple questions to get to know who he or she is *today*. Here are some examples:

• *Ask about favorites:* What is your favorite food? Color? Game? TV show? School subject? Car? Band? Sports star? Friend?

• *Ask about activities:* What do you like to do at recess? What do you like to do with your friends? What do you like to do with the family?

• *Ask about memories:* What did you do while I was away that you really enjoyed? What did you do that you really disliked? Would you tell me about your birthday party? School play? Soccer season?

Showing a clear interest in your child after a long separation can go a long way toward restoring the relationship. It's important to recognize that children experience the prolonged absence of a close adult differently, depending on their age, the closeness of the relationship before the absence, and the level of support that they received from remaining family members and close friends. Although most children are highly resilient, adjusting to an extended separation from a loved one can be hard, and some develop problems that don't simply disappear the moment you return. Knowing the reactions to separation that are common at different ages can help you to understand and respond better to your child, identify problems, and determine if and when to seek professional help.

HELPING YOUR TODDLER OR PRESCHOOLER ADJUST

Between the ages of 2 and 4, a great deal of children's energy is focused on communicating. Although you may believe that they're too young to understand or be affected by the absence of an adult, they actually are at an age when prolonged separations can be devastating. However, in that in-between stage when they comprehend many more words than they can speak, toddlers and preschoolers tend to express themselves in a variety of ways and often feel very frustrated when the adults around them don't "understand." One immediate reaction that toddler and preschool-age children commonly have to being separated from an important adult is to become more "clingy" with the adults who remain. A child who had once happily gone to preschool may now cling desperately to his or her parent, concerned that they too will leave and not return. Then, after a deployed parent returns, a young child may want to be in constant physical contact to ensure that he or she does not leave again. This level of clinginess may be difficult for a returning veteran who, in spite of enjoying the affection and time with his or her child, also needs alone-time to digest war-zone experiences and readjust to life at home.

A greater cause for concern for a returning veteran may be the young child who's distant and withdrawn and appears not to know his or her own parent or previously close family member. It may be that you were deployed at a time when your child was an infant and only just developing relationships. If this is true, then you may indeed be, in a sense, a stranger to your child, a person whom he or she knows only through photographs, video conferencing, and whatever else the remaining family might have shared about you. In this case, you may need to actually "introduce" yourself into your child's life in a gradual way, allowing for times of distance and clinging to other more-familiar adults until he or she gets to know you as a stable and integral member of the family. For preschool-age children who were older at the time of your deployment, the memory of a loved and needed family member's suddenly vanishing from their lives may cause them to be quite cautious and distant on your return. After all, they don't have the ability to understand why you left and don't trust that you can truly be depended on to be there when they need you. While you were away, remaining family members may have told you how your child had asked about you every day and frequently repeated phrases like "Daddy's away at the Army." Your child may even have played incessantly with toy soldiers or repeatedly had "Baby doll" left alone at home while Mommy and Daddy doll "went away." Because children at this age have particular difficulty using language to express their feelings and concerns, they instead act out many of their worries through their play.

For many young children, sudden and lengthy separations from an important adult can lead to new or intensified fears. It is not uncommon for preschool-age children to develop a sudden fear of the dark, strangers, or certain animals after a close adult has been deployed. These fears may come from children's concerns that they will no longer be as safe or protected as they were when the deployed parent was home. Of course, children aren't entirely aware of the reason for their concerns, and are even more limited in their ability to communicate them. Instead, they may create scary "monsters" to give a shape and name to their fear. Even after you return, your child may continue to fear the "monster under the bed" as he or she fears the possibility of waking up with you gone again. The important thing is that you take your child's concerns seriously. It's your job to be the "monster slayer" and do everything in your power to protect and keep your child safe. Ask your child what you can do to help "make the monster go away." Reassure him or her that you understand these concerns and are "back on the job" of being the protector.

While some children express their feelings through play or imaginary monsters, others may simply begin acting differently. During your deployment, you may have heard from a discouraged partner that your child had begun wetting the bed again after a successful transition out of diapers. Or your child may have begun asking for a bottle or reverted back to thumbsucking. Alternatively, your partner may have told you about how increasingly difficult it had become to manage your child or how your previously gentle son had been sent home from preschool for throwing rocks at other children. It's not uncommon for children to react to separation from an important adult by regressing back to things that they did when they were younger, particularly comforting things like carrying a favorite blanket or using a pacifier. It's also quite common for children to feel angry about being separated from their parent and to express their anger by disobedience or aggression.

For instance, a child who's missing his father may be jealous and aggressive toward another child whose daddy comes to pick him up at preschool. Another child may disobey her mother in the hopes that Daddy, who was the disciplinarian in the family, will come home to make sure that she follows the rules. Now that you're home, these behaviors may continue until your child is secure that you're there to care for him or her. For children who have reverted back to earlier behaviors such as bedwetting, it's important that you not punish them, but that you remind them of how they were able to stay dry through the night (or stop sucking their thumb) before and that you know they will soon be able to do it again.

Again, ask if there's anything that you can do to help them. If your child has become disobedient or aggressive, the most important thing that you can do is to be firm and consistent. The best way to help your child feel secure again is to provide structure and routine that he or she can depend on.

HELPING YOUR ELEMENTARY SCHOOL–AGE CHILD ADJUST

The biggest difference between preschool- and elementary school–age children is the ability to understand and communicate. Children between the ages of 5 and 12 are more aware of what they see and hear on television news, they discuss current events in school, and their friends are more likely to know what their parents do for a living and when a parent is absent. Elementary school–age children therefore know much more about the dangers of war and may have serious worries about the safety of the parent or loved one who has been deployed. Because they're becoming increasingly able to express their emotions, they may begin to use words like "hate" to communicate their anger, or may tell you that they're sad. But this is an age when children are most likely to experience their emotions physically. They may complain about stomachaches or headaches, have difficulty sleeping, or have a loss of appetite.

Elementary school–age children can also become whiny or moody or highly active when they experience the stress of separation and concern for the safety of a loved one. Like preschoolers, they may also revert back to earlier behaviors such as "baby-talk" or may be clingy and refuse to go to school because they fear being separated from their parent or caregiver. Younger children may want a night-light again or may insist on sleeping with the door open.

As with preschoolers, these behaviors may continue after you've returned home, and your child may simply need time to begin to feel secure that you're safe and can be depended on to take care of him or her. One way to help your child begin to feel more secure is to avoid exposing him or her to reminders of the war. This includes limiting your child's exposure to news, television programs, or movies about the war.

If your child asks, answer questions about the war and your absence honestly, but don't dwell on frightening details or allow the subject to dominate family time. If you do choose to let your child see war information on television, keep it brief, watch it with your child, and talk to your child afterward to help avoid misperceptions. Helping your child feel safe also includes limiting exposure to adult conversations about the war or related events. Remember—even when you think they're not listening or can't understand, they often are and do.

To help your child adjust to the changes that have occurred in the family since your return, as much as possible maintain the family routines that were established while you were away, particularly around sleeping, eating, and extracurricular activities. Be sure the bedtime routine includes tucking them in and reassuring children that they're safe. Above all, encourage your children to express their emotions, and be sure to spend time cuddling. Provide soothing and family-oriented activities, such as reading books, listening to music, taking a walk, or riding bikes, and try to lower your expectations temporarily about school performance and household chores.

HELPING YOUR MIDDLE OR HIGH SCHOOL–AGE CHILD ADJUST

If you think back on your own teenage years, you'll recall that adolescence is a hard time, regardless of your circumstances. But when a parent or a loved one is away for an extended period of time, a sensitive teenager can feel lost and confused, not knowing whom to trust or turn to. It's not uncommon for teenage children of deployed parents to have difficulty both at school and in relationships. They may have problems concentrating and may lack the motivation they once had to do well in school. A teenager may have significant concerns about your safety while at war, and these concerns may spread to worries about violence or death in general. They may become fascinated with death and the gruesome details of the war, or they may become distrustful of people who are "different," particularly those whom they see as the "enemy."

Teenagers who are in distress may act out in different ways. They may begin to use drugs or alcohol, or may take risks such as reckless driving or engaging in risky sexual behavior. They may skip school, quit their job, or refuse to do their usual chores. It's also quite common for distressed teenagers to become depressed and withdrawn, spending much of their time alone and in bed. Some may even have thoughts of suicide. They may engage in excessive video game playing or watching TV. It's important that you address aggressive, self-destructive, or risky behaviors by quickly setting limits and having firm and consistent expectations. Be aware that some teenagers are extremely skillful at acting out in a way in which *your response* to their behavior becomes the problem—not *their behavior* itself. If your teenager's behavior is severe or if he or she doesn't respond to limits, seek professional help. You should also seek help if your teenager is depressed and unable to accept support, or if he or she repeatedly talks about death or dying.

As with any elementary school–age children, it's important to help teenagers feel safe and secure by responding to their questions in limited detail and protecting them from being exposed to unnecessary violence or the gruesome details of war. Be sure that your teenager is receiving a balanced diet and enough rest. They may also benefit by spending extra time with friends. If this is the case, don't withdraw but, rather, get to know their friends. Learning about their friends will give you greater understanding about who your child is and how to be a better parent.

Encourage your child to express his or her feelings. Many teenagers benefit from writing in a journal or expressing their emotions through art. Be careful to respect their privacy (unless they're significantly acting out, in which case you may need to monitor their behavior more closely) and to listen patiently to their opinions, regardless of whether you agree. Listening to teenagers doesn't mean solving their problems or making their decisions for them. You may simply suggest that your teen delay making important decisions until he or she is feeling more settled. Again, family activities and routine plus lots of affection (yes—even teenagers need hugs!) can go a long way toward helping your child adjust to your return.

DECIDING WHEN TO SEEK PROFESSIONAL HELP FOR YOUR CHILD

You should seek help for your child if:

- Three to four months have gone by and you don't feel that your child's behavior has improved.
- Your child's symptoms seem severe (for example, having suicidal thoughts, using drugs or alcohol significantly, engaging in dangerous activities).
- Your child's ability to function at school or at home is significantly affected.

DISCIPLINING YOUR CHILDREN

Now that you're home, you may be eager to resume the duties and responsibilities that were yours before your time overseas, especially rule-setting and disciplining your children. In the war zone, everything you did was strictly regimented. You may have been in a position of authority, giving orders on a regular basis and expecting them to be followed to the letter. Compared to the orderliness of the military, your family life now seems chaotic and unruly.

In fact, your children could very well be less disciplined than they were before your deployment. While you were away you may have received reports from your partner of Johnny's bad behavior or Latoya's refusing to do her chores. Your child may have started "acting out" because of the way your absence changed the family structure, or there may be other issues.

Try to understand your child's actions. Sometimes asking children directly about their behavior can provide an explanation. But many children, especially those younger than 8, won't be able to answer you directly about why they're acting out, so you'll need to watch for other clues. Allow some leeway with your children when you first return. Acting-out behavior will often melt away with the right amount of parental structure and consistency. Put limits on behavior that makes problems for the family, and reward behavior that helps the family.

Whether you were the primary disciplinarian before your deployment or you and your partner were codisciplinarians, you should take at least two to three months after your return to fully step back into that role. Before you rush into Enforcer mode, though, consider a few suggestions that can make the transition more effective and less prone to failure.

OBSERVE

The first step in disciplining your children is to observe the family interactions. Watch how discipline is presently occurring (or not) in your family. Notice what's working and where you think problems may lie. It may be useful to take notes about your observations.

DISCUSS

When you sit down to talk with your partner, lead off with a positive observation before mentioning whatever problems you've noticed. Remind your partner that you're really impressed with how hard she or he has worked at taking care of the kids and how difficult it must have been to parent solo while you were away. From there, you can lead into your observations of what's working and what could use improvement when it comes to discipline. Review with your partner ideas you have for family rules, and come to an agreement on a discipline strategy. You may not exactly agree on everything, but as long as you and your partner are on the same page it will communicate to your children a sense that you're a team. That can reassure them and lead to less acting out. Talk about how you might best step back into the role of a disciplining parent.

When you and your partner have come to an agreement, discuss the rules with your children. Speak in a loving-parent way, not as the drill sergeant or C.O. you once were. Present your children with a clear statement of any new rules, including the consequences and rewards that come with them. Remember, children fare best when they have clear rules and consistent structure. Otherwise they can become anxious and overwhelmed.

REBUILD YOUR RELATIONSHIPS

Before promoting yourself to the position of supreme authority, spend time getting to know your children. The stronger your relationships are, the easier disciplining your children will be. Your child may have gained a surprising amount of maturity while you were away, and he or she may need more independence as well as more responsibility. If your children are now in their teens, ask them what they think are reasonable privileges and expectations for their age, and help them to understand the reason for the rules or restrictions you lay down.

LET YOUR PARTNER LEAD AT FIRST

Having your partner take the lead in disciplinary matters is a good strategy, because it lets you ease into your role little by little. You may be primed to overreact as a result of your war-zone experiences, military-based expectations, or the problem behaviors you heard about while you were away. Easing in will also help you get acquainted with the new culture in the house. At first, coordinate your efforts at disciplining the children with those of your partner. This will slow the process down. It may mean making an extra phone call or delaying your response to a child's behavior. But in the long run it will prove to be a useful strategy. As you become more involved, you and your partner can implement discipline together. Finally, move into the role of disciplinarian.

REVIEW HOW YOU AND YOUR PARTNER HANDLED PARTICULAR SITUATIONS

Whether you dealt with a problem solo or acted as a tag team in responding to your children's behavior, it's always good to spend time together thinking through how you handled the situation to see whether the two of you disagree about anything that was done and discuss how you might improve your parenting. Parents, just like children, are always works in progress.

USE POSITIVE AS WELL AS NEGATIVE CONSEQUENCES

Children do better when you provide structure by motivating good behavior instead of just punishing bad actions. Talk to your children to find out what they might be eager to work toward, and be sure your expectations are reasonable in terms of both time and effort. Be sure to provide small, spur-of-the-moment rewards such as going to a favorite park, as well as larger planned rewards like going to a sports event for continued good behavior. Above all, don't use family time or one-on-one time with you as either a reward or a punishment. Children's relationships with their parents and family should never be used as a disciplinary tool.

ALLOW FOR EXCEPTIONS TO THE RULE

Obviously, family situations may arise that call for different approaches. There may be times when someone could get hurt if you didn't respond quickly. In these situations you need to do everything you can to keep your children safe. But most parenting situations involving your children will be ones that can wait for you and your partner to discuss them before responding.

TIPS FOR PARENTS OF RETURNING VETERANS

While your son or daughter was in Iraq or Afghanistan, you were probably glued to the TV or were continually reading the newspaper or Internet accounts trying to find out what was happening to your child. Perhaps you stopped following the war in the media and only received communication directly from your son or daughter. Maybe you provided and received support from other families who also had loved ones overseas. During the time your child was deployed, you probably knew or heard of service men or women who didn't make it home to their families. The fear of uniformed service men or women walking up to your house with bad news still sends a shiver down your spine.

Luckily, you find yourself feeling incredibly relieved and fortunate that your child has made it home. But now that the celebration is over, what can you do to help ease your child's transition from the war to home? If you've noticed that your child is having trouble now that he or she is home but you're unsure how to help, the following tips might be useful. The appropriateness of these tips depends on a number of factors, including your relationship with your child, his or her age, and the degree to which he or she desires help.

• Let your son or daughter know what your concerns are by giving examples of specific things that they've done or said that you've observed. The more specific you are in your description of the be-haviors that concern you, the more difficult it will be for your child to deny the problem. Don't get into an argument with your child about whether he or she should seek treatment. Express your concerns and offer to help, but don't push, because he or she may rebel (after all, no matter what the age, he or she will always be your child!). In some situations it may be best to state your concerns and then back off. Provide your child with this book, along with other useful materials. Remember to allow your child time to come to the idea of getting help on his or her own. But if you believe your child is going to hurt himself, herself, or somebody else, dial 911 or turn to your local hospital's psychiatric emergency room for immediate help. *Don't wait.*

- Become an expert in the area of resources. Your child will need time to adjust to his or her life at home and may not be able to quickly tap into available resources and services. He or she may be initially too irritable or uninterested in seeking help to even find out what resources are available. Knowing where to direct your child for various services may help to smooth the transition.

- Have an honest discussion with your child about his or her financial situation. He or she may be reluctant or embarrassed to discuss finances with you but it may also help you understand some of the stress your child is experiencing. Let your child know that whatever financial difficulties are in the way, you are there to listen and help.

- Call your local Vet Center, Veterans Administration Medical Center (VA hospital), or local VA community-based outpatient clinic and speak with a therapist to get some ideas about how to bring up the idea of getting help for your child.

- Use the connections you may have developed while your child was away. Through meetings or e-mail listservs, you may be able to work with others to develop strategies that will help your child transition more easily.

- Give your child the opportunity to talk about his or her war experiences. Let him or her know you're willing to listen and that you won't make judgments or comments about what happened during deployment. If you've been to war or through your own traumatic experiences, you may discover that this is an opportunity to deepen your connection with your son or daughter by sharing your experience.

• Have a veteran of a previous war, or a veteran of Iraq or Afghanistan, come speak with your child to encourage him or her to seek help. Sometimes hearing how help has been beneficial from someone who had a similar problem can break through any denial your child may have.

Resources

This section lists websites and books where you'll find further information on problems or issues raised in this book. Because many of the websites offer information on more than one topic, as well as links to other sites that might be of interest, you can use these references as a starting point for a broader search.

While we've done our best to create a comprehensive list of resources here, other sources exist and new ones are created all the time. Keep in mind that information found on the Internet is not always reliable or up-to-date. The authors of *Courage After Fire* are not responsible for the content provided on the websites listed below. Always double-check the accuracy of any website's information through other sources. Since websites change continually, please note that the following information is current as of September 1, 2005.

ALCOHOL USE

Al-Anon/Alateen
www.al-anon.alateen.org
888-425-2666
This organization offers hope and support to the families and friends of alcoholics.

Alcoholics Anonymous

www.alcoholics-anonymous.org

This is the largest and most well-known international self-help based organization of recovering alcoholics. You can locate meetings in your area by navigating this website.

Books to read

Fletcher, Anne. *Sober for Good: New Solutions for Drinking Problems—Advice from Those Who Have Succeeded.* Houghton Mifflin, 2002.

Tate, Phillip. *Alcohol: How to Give It Up and Be Glad You Did.* See Sharp Press, 1996.

AMPUTEES

Limbless Association

www.limbless-association.org/search/default.asp

This association helps limbless individuals of all ages achieve maximum mobility and independence in home, hospital, education, employment, and the community. It also offers help to caregivers of limbless individuals.

National Amputation Foundation (NAF)

www.nationalamputation.org

Founded in 1919, this association offers assistance such as peer counseling, support, and referral information to American war veterans who are amputees.

Books to read

Riley, Richard. *Living with a Below-Knee Amputation: A Unique Insight from a Prosthetist/Amputee.* Slack, 2005.

Sabolich, John. *You're Not Alone: With the Personal Stories of 38 Amputees.* Sabolich Prosthetic & Research Center, 1993.

ANGER

www.apa.org/pubinfo/anger.html

This website provides information on anger and anger management from the American Psychological Association.

Books to read

McKay, Mathew, & Rogers, Peter. *The Anger Control Workbook*. New Harbinger Publications, 2000.

Reilly, Patrick. *Anger Management for Substance Abuse and Mental Health Clients: A Cognitive Behavioral Manual*. Diane Publishing Co., 2003.

ANXIETY

www.algy.com/anxiety/anxiety.php

This website claims to be the oldest Internet resource offering services and support for those who suffer from anxiety and panic attacks. It provides information about anxiety disorders and support through chat rooms with other anxiety sufferers.

Books to read

Barlow, David, & Craske, Michelle. *Mastery of Your Anxiety and Panic: Map-3 (Treatments That Work)* (3rd Edition). Oxford University Press, 2005.

Bourne, Edmund. *The Anxiety and Phobia Workbook*. New Harbinger Publications, 2005.

Bourne, Edmund, Brownstein, Arlen, & Garano, Lorna. *Natural Relief for Anxiety: Complementary Strategies for Easing Fear, Panic and Worry*. New Harbinger Publications, 2004.

Lark, Susan. *Dr. Susan Lark's Anxiety and Stress Self Help Book: Effective Solutions for Nervous Tension, Emotional Distress, Anxiety and Panic*. Celestial Arts, 1996.

CHILD ABUSE PREVENTION

www.childhelpusa.org/programs_hotline.htm
800-422-4453
This website offers, among other services, a 24-hour hotline to help locate resources in your area for children who are abused or at risk of being abused.

CHILD HEALTH AND DEVELOPMENT

American Academy of Pediatrics
www.aap.org/topics.html
This organization is made up of pediatricians interested in providing information on physical, mental, and social health for infants, children, adolescents, and young adults.

Kids Health
www.kidshealth.org/index.html
This organization provides information about child physical and emotional health from before birth through adolescence, including separate areas for parents, kids, and teens.

Books to read

Kindlon, Dan, & Thompson, Michael. *Raising Cain: Protecting the Emotional Life of Boys.* Ballantine Press, 1999.

Lieberman, Alicia. *The Emotional Life of the Toddler.* The Free Press, 1993.

Pipher, Mary. *Reviving Ophelia: Saving the Selves of Adolescent Girls.* Ballantine Books, 1994.

Sears, James; Sears, Martha; Sears, Robert, & Sears, William. *The Baby Book: Everything You Need to Know About Your Baby from Birth to Age Two* (Revised and Updated Edition). Little, Brown, 2003.

Seligman, Martin. *The Optimistic Child: Proven Program to Safeguard Children from Depression and Build Lifelong Resilience.* Harper Paperbacks, 1996.

Stern, Daniel. *Diary of a Baby: What Your Child Sees, Feels and Experiences*. Basic Books, 1990.

Taffel, Ron. *Nurturing Good Children Now*. Golden Books, 1999.

COUNSELING

Department of Veterans Affairs Medical Centers (VA Medical Centers)

www.seamlesstransition.va.gov

This is the VA's main website for veterans returning from Iraq and Afghanistan. You can locate your local VA office or hospital through this website.

Military ONESOURCE

www.militaryonesource.com

800-342-9647

This organization provides various kinds of services, including brief counseling to veterans and their families if the veteran is still on active duty. Reservists and National Guard personnel can use this organization if they're still on active duty.

National Alliance for the Mentally Ill (NAMI)

www.nami.org

This organization provides support and advocacy for consumers, families, and friends of people with severe mental illnesses.

Veterans Center Readjustment Counseling Service (Vet Center)

www.va.gov/rcs/index.htm

These centers, which are often staffed by veterans, are located throughout the country and provide a variety of services, including counseling to veterans and their families.

DEPARTMENT OF DEFENSE

http://deploymenthealthlibrary.fhp.osd.mil/home.jsp

This website, maintained by the Department of Defense, provides service members, families, and health care providers a wealth of information about deployment and reintegration.

THE FOLLOWING ARE THE PRIMARY WEBSITES FOR THE ARMED FORCES:

Air Force
www.af.mil

Army
www.army.mil

Coast Guard
www.uscg.mil/USCG.shtm

National Guard
www.ngb.army.mil

Navy
www.navy.mil

Marines
www.usmc.mil/marinelink/mcn2000.nsf/frontpagenews

Marine for Life
www.m4l.usmc.mil/portal/server.pt

This program is for Marines helping other Marines transition to civilian life. It's for all Marines, including those who have been injured and their families. Navy personnel who served with or in direct support of Marines are also eligible to receive services.

RESERVE WEBSITES:

Air Force Reserve
www.afreserve.com

Army
www.armyreserve.army.mil/usar/home

Coast Guard Reserve
www.uscg.mil/hq/reserve/reshmpg.html

Marine Corp Reserve
www.marforres.usmc.mil

Navy Reserve
www.navalreserve.com/ps

Department of Veterans Affairs (VA)
www.va.gov

This is the main website for the VA. It's a great place to begin your search if you're interested in any VA services.

GI Bill
www.gibill.va.gov
800-442-4551

This website provides detailed information on the GI Bill, such as eligibility and education benefits.

Military Severely Injured Joint Support Operations Center
888-774-1361

This center advocates for severely injured military personnel and their families.

Seamless Transition Homepage
www.seamlesstransition.va.gov

This is the VA's main website for veterans returning from Iraq and Afghanistan. You can locate your local VA through this website.

Veterans Benefits Administration
www.vba.va.gov

This is the main website of the Veterans Benefits Administration. It gives information on compensation and pension, home loans, and other services.

Veterans Center Readjustment Counseling Service (Vet Center)

www.va.gov/rcs/index.htm

These centers, which are often staffed by veterans, are located throughout the country and provide a variety of services, including counseling to veterans and their families.

Vocational Rehabilitation and Employment Service

www.vba.va.gov/bln/vre/index.htm

This website provides information on rehabilitation, education counseling, employment counseling, and independent living services for veterans.

DEPLOYMENT

Ameriforce Deployment Guide

www.deploymentguide.com

This guide provides valuable information on deployment for veterans and their families.

www.armyfrg.org/skins/ArmyFRG/display.aspx

This website is designed to improve online communication between deployed soldiers and their families.

DEPRESSION

www.allaboutdepression.com/about.html

This website is devoted to providing the general public with accurate information on depression.

www.dbsalliance.org

This organization provides information about depression and bipolar disorder and organizes support groups across the country.

Books to read

Burns, David. *The Feeling Good Handbook*. New York: Penguin Books, 1989.

Copeland, Mary Ellen. *The Depression Workbook: A Guide for Living with Depression and Manic Depression*. New Harbinger Publications, 2002.

Golant, Mitch, & Golant, Susan. *What to Do When Someone You Love Is Depressed*. Owl Books, New York, 1998.

Greenberger, Dennis, & Padesky, Christine. *Mind Over Mood: Change How You Feel by Changing the Way You Think*. New York. Guilford Press, 1995.

DOMESTIC VIOLENCE

Elder Abuse Hotline
800-879-6682
endabuse.org/about
This hotline helps elders who are being abused.

National Council on Child Abuse and Family Violence
www.nccafv.org
This nonprofit resource center is dedicated to preventing family violence. It provides a hotline and education materials on family violence.

Family Violence Prevention Fund
www.endabuse.org
The Family Violence Prevention Fund works to prevent violence against women and children around the world.

National Domestic Violence Hotline
800-799-7233
This hotline helps those facing domestic violence.

Books to read

Kubany, Edward, McCraig, Mari, & Laconsay, Janet. *Healing the Trauma of Domestic Violence: A Workbook for Women*. New Harbinger Publications, 2004.

DRUG ABUSE

Narcotics Anonymous
www.na.org
818-773-9999

This is the largest and most well-known international self-help organization for recovering drug addicts. You can locate meetings in your area by navigating this website.

National Institute of Health
www.nlm.nih.gov/medlineplus/drugabuse.html

This website provides information from the National Institute of Health on drug abuse. You can navigate from this website to other websites addressing a variety of health- and mental-health related questions.

Books to read

Perkinson, Robert. *The Alcoholism and Drug Abuse Patient Workbook*. Sage Publications, 2003.

EDUCATION

Air Force Aid Society
www.afas.org/body_grant.htm

This website provides information on education grants available to Air Force members and their families.

DOD Voluntary Education Programs
www.voled.doded.mil/voled_web/voledhome.asp

This website provides information about education programs for active duty military. Every year more than 300,000 service men and women participate in this program.

FinAid
www.finaid.org/military

Established in 1994, FinAid is a comprehensive website of financial aid information that can link you to additional financial aid resources and materials for veterans.

GI Bill

www.gibill.va.gov

800-442-4551

This website provides detailed information on the GI Bill, such as eligibility and education benefits for veterans.

Navy-Marine Corps Relief Society

www.nmcrs.org/education

This organization provides need-based education scholarships to Navy and Marine Corps families.

State Government

There are services for veterans and their families that are funded through each state. Some of these resources may include tuition waivers or deductions for your children and home loans. Check your state's veterans resources for more information. Here is an example from the state of California:

California Department of Veterans Affairs

www.cdva.ca.gov/default.asp

EMPLOYMENT

Check with your state's Employment Development Department to learn more about services for veterans.

Destiny Group

www.destinygroup.com/destiny/contact/aboutus.jsp

This private organization offers veterans and their spouses employment-related services, such as instruction in résumé building, job interview preparation, and job placement assistance.

Federal Service

www.usajobs.opm.gov

This website lists federal jobs throughout the world.

Helmets to Hardhats

www.helmetstohardhats.org/home.jsp

Launched in 2003, Helmets to Hardhats helps to place military service members in construction field careers.

Hire Veterans.com
www.hireveterans.com
This website provides extensive employment opportunities and résumé posting.

Military Exits
www.militaryexits.com
This website helps employers find qualified veterans for employment.

Military Spouse Career Center
www.military.com/spouse
This center provides job opportunities for the spouses of active duty military.

National Committee for Employer Support of the Guard and Reserve
www.esgr.com
This website's mission is to "gain and maintain active support from all public and private employers for the men and women of the National Guard and Reserve as defined by demonstrated employer commitment to employee military service."

Troops to Teachers
www.dantes.doded.mil/dantes_web/troopstoteachers/index.htm?flag=True
Established in 1994 as a Department of Defense program, this organization helps recruit teachers for schools that serve low-income students.

United States Department of Labor
www.dol.gov/dol/topic/hiring/veterans.htm

The Veteran Employment and Training Service (VETS), part of the Department of Labor, has a mission to "provide veterans with the resources and services to succeed in the 21st century workforce...."

United States Office of Personnel Management
www.opm.gov/employ/html/vetguide.htm
This is the federal government's guide to veterans' preference for employment.

Vet Jobs.com
www.vetjobs.com
A full-service job and résumé posting website that was founded by two former Navy officers with the belief that veterans have the skills it takes to perform in the workforce.

Veteran Employment
www.veteranemployment.com
Working cooperatively with Monster.com, this website allows you to search for jobs, including jobs with security clearance.

Books to read
Bolles, Richard, & Bolles, Mark. *What Color Is Your Parachute? 2005: A Practical Manual for Job-Hunters and Career-Changers*. Ten Speed Press, 2004.

Lore, Nicholas. *The Pathfinder: How to Choose or Change Your Career for a Lifetime of Satisfaction and Success*. Fireside, 1998.

EMPLOYMENT RIGHTS AND LAW

www.coworkforce.com/VET/?vrr.asp
This website from the Colorado Department of Labor and Employment outlines the Uniformed Services Employment Rights Act (USERRA) and your rights regarding returning to a job held before deployment.

FEDERAL GOVERNMENT: CONTACTS FOR THE US CONGRESS

www.senate.gov

This website provides information about all 100 US senators, including their e-mail and mailing addresses.

www.house.gov

This website provides information about all 435 US representatives, including their e-mail and mailing addresses.

GRIEF

www.griefnet.org

This website offers an Internet community of persons dealing with grief, death, and major loss.

www.istss.org/publications/pamphlets.htm

Founded in 1985, the purpose of the International Society of Traumatic Stress Studies (ISTSS) is to share information about the effects of trauma. This website provides detailed information on trauma, loss, and traumatic grief.

Books to read

Noel, Brook, & Blair, Pamela. *I Wasn't Ready to Say Goodbye: Surviving, Coping and Healing after the Sudden Death of a Loved One.* Champion Press, 2000.

HEALTH

www.hooah4health.com

This is a US Army–sponsored health promotion and wellness website. Unlike other health-related websites, this one is specifically designed to address the health protection and readiness requirements of the Army, particularly its Reserve component.

www.webmd.com

This website provides extensive information on general health.

Books to read

Carlson, Karen, Eisenstat, Stephanie, & Ziporyn, Terra. *The New Harvard Guide to Women's Health*. Belknap Press, 2004.

Simon, Harvey. *The Harvard Medical School Guide to Men's Health: Lessons from the Harvard Men's Health Studies*. Free Press, 2004.

IRAQ WAR VETERANS ORGANIZATION

www.iraqwarveterans.org/index.html

This organization's mission is to represent veterans who served in Iraq.

MILITARY SEXUAL TRAUMA

Men and Sexual Trauma

www.ncptsd.va.gov/facts/specific/fs_male_sexual_assault.html

This website provides information from the National Center for PTSD about the effects of sexual assault on men.

Women and Sexual Trauma

www.ncptsd.va.gov/facts/specific/fs_female_sex_assault.html

This website provides information from the National Center for PTSD about the effects of sexual assault on women.

Books to read

Matsakis, Aphrodite. *The Rape Recovery Handbook: Step-by-Step Help for Survivors of Sexual Assault*. New Harbinger Publications, 2003.

NATIONAL MILITARY FAMILY ASSOCIATION

www.nmfa.org/site/PageServer?pagename=op_default

This organization advocates for improvement in the quality of military life.

NEUROLOGY INFORMATION

www.neurologychannel.com/tbi

This website provides information about traumatic brain injury and neurology.

NEUROPSYCHOLOGY INFORMATION

www.neuropsychologycentral.com

This website provides information about traumatic brain injury and neuropsychology.

PAIN

www.painfoundation.org

This organization is dedicated to eliminating the undertreatment of pain in America.

Books to read

Caudill-Slosberg, Margaret. *Managing Pain Before It Manages You* (Revised Edition). Guilford Press, 2001.

PANIC

www.algy.com/anxiety/index.php

This website claims to be the oldest Internet resource offering information, services, and support (including chat rooms) for those who suffer from anxiety and panic.

Books to read

Barlow, David, & Craske, Michelle. *Mastery of Your Anxiety and Panic: Map-3 (Treatments That Work)* (3rd Edition). Oxford University Press, 2005.

Carbonell, David. *Panic Attacks Workbook: A Guided Program for Breaking the Panic Trick.* Ulysses Press, 2004.

PARENTS AND PARENTING

Marine Parents
www.marineparents.com
This website provides support to Marine mothers, fathers, spouses, families, and friends.

Soldiers and Families Middle East Resource
www.campdoha.org/index.htm
This website provides information about the Middle East to service members and their families, friends, and supporters.

Veterans and Families Coming Home
www.veteransandfamilies.org/page/page/1325329.htm
This website was created to provide community support to veterans, their families, and employers; to mobilize subject experts to study the psychological issues involved in readjustment; and to furnish research findings to assist service providers.

Books to read

Jordan, Pamela, Stanley, Scott, & Markman, Howard. *Becoming Parents: How to Strengthen Your Marriage as Your Family Grows.* Jossey-Bass, 1999.

Kindlon, Dan, & Thompson, Michael. *Raising Cain: Protecting the Emotional Life of Boys.* Ballantine Press, 1999.

Lieberman, Alicia. *The Emotional Life of the Toddler.* Free Press, 1993.

Pipher, Mary. *Reviving Ophelia: Saving the Selves of Adolescent Girls.* Ballantine Books, 1994.

Runkel, Hal Edward. *ScreamFree Parenting: Raising Your Kids by Keeping Your Cool (Screamfree Living).* Oakmont Publishing, 2005.

Sears, James, Sears, Martha; Sears, Robert, & Sears, William. *The Baby Book: Everything You Need to Know about Your Baby from Birth to Age Two* (Revised and Updated Edition). Little, Brown, 2003.

Seligman, Martin. *The Optimistic Child: Proven Program to Safeguard Children from Depression and Build Lifelong Resilience.* Harper Paperbacks, 1996.

Sells, Scott. *Parenting Your Out-of-Control Teenager.* St. Martins Press, 2001.

Stern, Daniel. *Diary of a Baby: What Your Child Sees, Feels and Experiences.* Basic Books, 1990.

Taffel, Ron. *Nurturing Good Children Now.* Golden Books, 1999.

PHOBIAS

www.nmha.org
The National Mental Health Association is the oldest and largest nonprofit organization focusing on mental health and illness. This website provides extensive information about phobias and other mental health problems.

Books to read
Bourne, Edmund. *The Anxiety and Phobia Workbook.* New Harbinger Publications, 2005.

POSTTRAUMATIC STRESS

David Baldwin's Trauma Pages
www.trauma-pages.com
This website provides information on trauma. Its primary audience is clinicians and researchers.

National Center for PTSD (NCPTSD)
www.ncptsd.va.gov
The National Center for PTSD was created in 1989 by Congress to address the needs of veterans diagnosed with military-related PTSD. This website provides extensive information on trauma for clinicians, veterans, and their families.

Books to read

Allen, Jon. *Coping with Trauma: Hope Through Understanding.* American Psychiatric Association, 2004.

Herman, Judith. *Trauma and Recovery.* Basic Books, 1997.

Johnson, Susan. *Emotionally Focused Couple's Therapy with Trauma Survivors: Strengthening Attachment Bonds.* Guilford Press, 2002.

Mason, Patience. *Recovering from the War: A Guide for All Veterans, Family Members, Friends and Therapists.* Patience Press, 1999.

Matsakis, Aphrodite. *I Can't Get Over It: A Handbook for Trauma Survivors.* New Harbinger Publications, 1996.

———. *Vietnam Wives.* Sidran Press, 1996

Schiraldi, Glenn R. *The Posttraumatic Stress Disorder Sourcebook.* Lowell House, 2000.

Williams, Mary Beth, & Poijula, Soili. *The PTSD Workbook: Simple Effective Techniques for Overcoming Traumatic Stress Symptoms.* New Harbinger Publications, 2002.

RELATIONSHIPS

www.gottman.com

The Gottman Institute website provides information on relationships and parenting.

www.prepinc.com/index.asp

This website provides resources that you can purchase to help improve your marriage.

Books to read

Christensen, Andrew, & Jacobson, Neil. *Reconcilable Differences.* Guilford Press, 2000.

Gottman, John. *The Relationship Cure: A 5-Step Guide to Strengthening Your Marriage, Family, and Friendships.* Three Rivers Press, 2002.

————. *The Seven Principles for Making Marriage Work.* Crown Publishers, 1999.

Jordan, Pamela, Stanley, Scott, & Markman, Howard. *Becoming Parents: How to Strengthen Your Marriage as Your Family Grows.* Jossey-Bass, 1999.

Markman, Howard, & Stanley, Scott. *Fighting for Your Marriage: Positive Steps for Preventing Divorce and Preserving a Lasting Love.* Jossey-Bass, 1994.

SELF-HELP (OR ADVOCACY)

National Alliance for the Mentally Ill (NAMI)
www.nami.org
This organization is a support and advocacy organization of consumers, families, and friends of people with severe mental illnesses.

National Mental Health Association
www.nmha.org/index.cfm
This organization addresses all aspects of mental health and mental illness through advocacy, education, and research.

SLEEP SPECIALISTS

American Academy of Sleep Medicine (AASM)
www.aasmnet.org/FactSheet.aspx
This website provides information from the American Academy of Sleep Medicine on sleep medicine and research. The AASM's mission is to "assure quality care for patients with sleep disorders, promote the advancement of sleep research and provide public and professional education."

National Sleep Foundation
www.sleepfoundation.org

This website provides an array of information from the National Sleep Foundation on sleep difficulties. The foundation is "dedicated to improving public health and safety by achieving understanding of sleep and sleep disorders, and by supporting education, sleep-related research, and advocacy."

Books to read

Jacobs, Gregg, & Benson, Herbert. *Say Good Night to Insomnia: The Six-Week, Drug-Free Program Developed at Harvard Medical School.* Owl Books, 1999.

Maas, James, & Wherry, Megan. *Power Sleep: The Revolutionary Program That Prepares Your Mind for Peak Performance.* Collins, 1999.

SUICIDE PREVENTION

USA National Suicide Hotlines
http://suicidehotlines.com
800-784-2433
800-273-8255

This website provides hotline phone numbers in every state for those persons thinking of suicide and their loved ones.

www.psycom.net/depression.central.suicide.html
This website is designed for those persons considering suicide and their loved ones.

Books to read

Quinnett, Paul. *Suicide: the Forever Decision: For Those Thinking about Suicide, and for Those Who Know, Love, or Counsel Them.* Crossroad Classic, 1987.

THERAPIST ORGANIZATIONS

These organizations have general mental health information and may provide you with a list of therapists in your community.

American Association of Marriage and Family Therapists
www.aamft.org/index_nm.asp

American Family Therapy Academy
www.afta.org/resources.html

American Psychiatric Association
www.psych.org

American Psychological Association
www.apa.org

Association for the Advancement of Behavior Therapy
www.aabt.org/clinical/clinical.htm

International Society of Traumatic Stress Studies
www.istss.org

National Association of Social Workers
www.naswdc.org

TRAUMATIC BRAIN INJURY

Brain Injury Association
800-444-6443
www.biausa.org/Pages/home.html
This organization provides advocacy, education, research, and
prevention information on traumatic brain injury.

Defense and Veterans Brain Injury Center
www.dvbic.org
800-870-9244
This program, administered jointly by both the Department
of Defense and the Department of Veterans Affairs, has a mission
to "serve active duty military, their dependents, and veterans with
traumatic brain injury through state of the art medical care, inno-
vative clinical research initiatives, and educational programs."

Traumatic Brain Injury Survival Guide

www.tbiguide.com

This easy-to-read guide was developed for survivors of traumatic brain injury and their families.

Books to read

Gottfried, Jean-Louis. *The Mild Traumatic Brain Injury Workbook: Your Program for Regaining Cognitive Function and Overcoming Emotional Pain*. New Harbinger Publications, 2004.

Gronwall, D. M. A., Wrightson, Philip, & Waddell, Peter. *Head Injury: The Facts: A Guide for Families and Care-Givers*. Oxford Medical Publications, 1998.

VETERAN SERVICES (NON-DVA)

These organizations provide a number of advocacy-related services for veterans with some providing assistance in filing for service-connected disability compensation ratings.

National Association of County Service Officers

www.nacvso.org

National Veterans Foundation

www.nvf.org

888-777-4443

This organization offers support and information for veterans and their families about resources available in the community, including crisis intervention, benefits counseling, medical treatment, food and shelter, legal aid, and employment training.

Salute America's Heroes

www.saluteheroes.org/redesign

This website offers help to military service members who have been wounded or disabled and their families.

Veterans Service Organizations

American Legion
www.legion.org

Am-Vets
www.amvets.org

Disabled American Veterans (DAV)
www.dav.org

Paralyzed Veterans of America
www.pva.org

Veterans of Foreign Wars (VFW)
www.vfw.org

VOLUNTEER ORGANIZATIONS

American Red Cross
www.redcross.org
This international nonprofit organization offers humanitarian aid to victims of natural and manmade disasters as well as support and comfort to military service members and their families. Volunteers can give donations and assistance.

Habitat for Humanity
www.habitat.org
This Christian nonprofit organization helps build housing for those in need. Volunteers can help build new homes.

Salvation Army
www.salvationarmyusa.org

This national nonprofit religious-based organization offers relief to those in need and provides opportunities for volunteers to contribute money, time, and resources.

United Way
national.unitedway.org
This national nonprofit organization is dedicated to making a measurable impact in underprivileged areas in America through community-based outreach, funding, and resources. Volunteers can give donations and assistance.

Volunteer Match
www.volunteermatch.org
This organization helps people find a place to volunteer.

Books to read
Blaustein, Arthur. *Make a Difference: America's Guide to Volunteering and Community Service.* Jossey-Bass, 2003.

Index

INDEX ✦ **231**

About the Authors

Keith Armstrong, L.C.S.W., is a clinical professor, Department of Psychiatry, University of California, San Francisco. He is Director of Couples and Family Therapy, Director of Mental Health Social Work, and a member of the Posttraumatic Stress Disorder Program at the San Francisco Department of Veterans Affairs Medical Center. He provides therapy for individuals, couples, families, and groups who have been exposed to traumatic events. In 1999 Armstrong was invited to Taiwan after an earthquake to provide education to professionals on how to intervene following a traumatic event. He has made numerous television and radio appearances as well as given interviews in newspaper articles discussing treatment of war stress, including PTSD. Armstrong was utilized as a PTSD expert on a nationally televised show on the History Channel and interviewed by Swiss Public Radio about returning veterans who served in Afghanistan and Iraq. He has written articles and chapters on debriefing after trauma and on the treatment of couples when one person has a diagnosis of PTSD. In 2000, 2003, 2004, and 2005, Armstrong won the UCSF Residents Department of Psychiatry award for excellence in teaching. He has a private practice in San Francisco, where he specializes in treating couples and families.

Suzanne Best, Ph.D., is a staff psychologist at the University of California, San Francisco and a research psychologist in the Posttraumatic Stress Disorder Research Program at the San Francisco Department of Veterans Affairs Medical Center. In her nine years with the PTSD Research Program, she has directed numerous studies of combat veterans and has coauthored numerous articles on trauma and PTSD in both civilians and military personnel. Currently she is engaged in developing and implementing cognitive behavioral treatments for Vietnam, Iraq, and Afghanistan veterans and is responsible for the training and weekly supervision of the therapists providing these treatments. In addition to her research activities, she has a clinical practice in Portland, Oregon, where she specializes in the treatment of emergency services personnel, returning veterans, and civilian victims of trauma and conducts privately retained forensic evaluations of traumatized individuals.

Paula Domenici, Ph.D., is currently a Congressional Fellow in Washington, DC, selected by the American Psychological Association through the American Association for the Advancement of Science. She was formerly a staff psychologist of the Posttraumatic Stress Disorder Program at the San Francisco Department of Veterans Affairs Medical Center. There she developed the clinical program for recently returning veterans from Iraq and Afghanistan and coordinated the mental health triaging for this group of veterans. She has provided individual and group therapy to these veterans as well as those from the Persian Gulf and Vietnam wars and World War II. She also spearheaded the support program for partners and spouses of veterans. Domenici has presented at various conferences on the reactions to war and readjustment concerns of returning troops.

Acknowledgments

I would like to thank my parents Robert and Priscilla Armstrong for teaching me how to persevere, my sister Sally Hermann for teaching me about courage, my wife Mia Laurence for her incredible support and her valuable input, my children Erin and Elijah for "allowing" Dad to go to work on the weekends, my father-in-law Michael Laurence for his thoughtful ideas, our neighbor Jenny Houston, and my work colleagues, Nancy Odell, L.C.S.W., and Frank Schoenfeld, M.D., for their suggestions and support.

Finally, I would like to thank the veterans and their families with whom I have worked for teaching me more about life than they will ever know.

—*Keith Armstrong*

• • •

First and foremost, I would like to express my gratitude to our newest veterans and the families who support them. I have appreciated the privilege of working with our nation's heroes and heroines and with this book I hope to give back some of what I have learned.

I would like to thank the veteran closest to my heart, my father, for inspiring me to enter this profession and for his continued wisdom and support. To my mother, thank you for your persistence in encouraging the writer in me and for always being there to lend an ear. My husband John, thank you for your patience and endurance, and simply for your love. And to my son Julian, your beautiful smile reminds me of what really matters.

—*Suzanne Best*

• • •

Working with veterans has been one of the most meaningful experiences in my life. Never have I felt as connected to a group of people as I have these veterans and their families. You have taught me that what is important in life is building and maintaining relationships and appreciating one another. Thank you for allowing me to give support to you during your times of need as you have given so generously to our country, each other, and me. You are wonderful people, and I will not forget your contributions. To those veterans returning from Iraq and Afghanistan, I hope this book will empower you to find more peace, stability, and happiness because you deserve only the best.

I am grateful to my sister Clare for motivating me to pursue a career in psychology. I also would like to thank my two biggest role models, my mother and father. You have made so many things possible for me through your hard work, humility, and compassion towards all kinds of people. From you, I have learned that small acts of kindness and justice can improve the lives of others and can create a ripple effect that leads to greater change.

— *Paula Domenici*

• • •

We would like to thank Ashley Chase and Richard Harris from Ulysses Press for believing in the mission of this book and having faith in us to complete it.

We are grateful to the following individuals for their special contributions to this book. The time and energy they have invested to help us is a reflection of their dedication to our returning troops: John Blankenship, M.A.; Gerard Choucroun, M.S.W.; Dawn Lawhon, Ph.D.; Shannon McCaslin, Ph.D.; Nancy O'Dell, L.C.S.W.; Polly Rose, L.C.S.W.; Vicky Steen.

The following researchers, clinicians, and authors have influenced some of the ideas we present in this book: David Barlow, Ph.D.; Herbert Benson, M.D.; Insoo Kim Berg, M.S.W.; Edmund Bourne, Ph.D.; Richard Bryant, Ph.D.; Daniella Cortez Cavenagh, Ph.D.; Michelle Craske, Ph.D.; Lorna Garano; John Gottman, Ph.D.; Judith Herman, M.D.; Neil Jacobson, Ph.D.; Sue Johnson, Ed.D.; Marsha Linehan, Ph.D.; James Maas, Ph.D.; I. Lisa McCann, Ph.D.; William Miller, Ph.D.; Lisa Najavits, Ph.D.; Laurie Pearlman, Ph.D.; Patrick Reilly, Ph.D.; Patricia Resick, Ph.D.; Karen Saakvitne, Ph.D.; Glenn Schiraldi, Ph.D.; Monica Schnike, Ph.D.; Catherine Shear, M.D.; Victoria Tichenor, Ph.D.